Dear Mom and Dad

ALSO BY PATTI DAVIS

Nonfiction

*Floating in the Deep End: How Caregivers Can See
Beyond Alzheimer's*

*The Wit and Wisdom of Gracie: An Opinionated Pug's
Guide to Life* (with Gracie Davis)

*The Lives Our Mothers Leave Us: Prominent Women
Discuss the Complex, Humorous, and Ultimately Loving
Relationships They Have with Their Mothers*

The Long Goodbye

Fiction

The Wrong Side of Night

The Blue Hour

Till Human Voices Wake Us

Bondage

Dear Mom and Dad

*A Letter about Family, Memory, and the
America We Once Knew*

PATTI DAVIS

LIVERIGHT PUBLISHING CORPORATION
A DIVISION OF W. W. NORTON & COMPANY
Independent Publishers Since 1923
NEW YORK   LONDON

For information about permission to reproduce selections
from this book, write to Permissions, Liveright Publishing
Corporation, a division of W. W. Norton & Company, Inc.,
500 Fifth Avenue, New York, NY 10110

For information about special discounts for bulk
purchases, please contact W. W. Norton Special Sales at
specialsales@wwnorton.com or 800-233-4830

Manufacturing by Lake Book Manufacturing
Production manager: Julia Druskin

Library of Congress Cataloging-in-Publication Data Available

ISBN 978-1-324-09348-0

Liveright Publishing Corporation
500 Fifth Avenue, New York, N.Y. 10110
www.wwnorton.com

W. W. Norton & Company Ltd.
15 Carlisle Street, London W1D 3BS

1 2 3 4 5 6 7 8 9 0

This book is dedicated to Robert Weil. Thank you for calling me with the idea. It's a story I had been wanting to tell and I am eternally grateful that you opened the door.

We honor our parents by carrying their best forward and laying the rest down. By fighting and taming the demons that laid them low and now reside in us.

—BRUCE SPRINGSTEEN,
Born to Run (2016)

Dear Mom and Dad

The street where we lived . . .

Dear Mom and Dad,

Our house has been torn down—the fifties mid-century modern that came to be known as the General Electric House. I watched it happen, returning to take walks in our old neighborhood— high in Pacific Palisades, far from the busyness of the city, with the ocean close enough that the air often smells like sea salt. The large tree that used to shade our deck was left—the tree you used to trim yourself, Dad. It remained for a while, pinned against the sky, until one day it was gone too. I still walk up there, in that place with so many memories. They've built a huge two-story house on the lot that was once ours, and many other homes on that short dead-end street have been demolished and

replaced with enormous mansions. There is construction everywhere. I can imagine, Dad, how you
would look around, raise one eyebrow in amusement, and probably question why anyone would
need such a big dwelling. "They'll get lost trying to
find the kitchen," I think you'd say. During these
walks, my mind travels back and forth between
what is literally around me and the memories of
what used to be.

It was on these neighborhood streets that I
learned to ride a bike. I would take our dog Lady,
a shepherd we rescued after we found her abandoned, and walk her to the end of the cul-de-sac
where the reclusive man who didn't like kids lived
behind a huge wooden gate, his house hidden in a
grove of oak trees. As I got older, I'd spend time on
these streets because they felt more peaceful than
our home did.

I'm seventy now, an age when most of us con-
template our mortality, look both ahead and behind
us, questioning what from the past still tugs on our
life, which memories haunt us, which ones sustain
us. In the past, I have journeyed as a writer far into
the terrain of autobiography, sometimes inappro-
priately so. But I've learned some things along the
way. I've learned that when it comes to exploring
our past, we're like archaeologists—scraping away

layers, searching for truths, hoping for treasures. That's basically true for everyone, which is the other thing I've learned. Whether or not a family is famous, there exists always a public perception and a private reality. Maybe it's the neighbors or a circle of friends and acquaintances who have opinions, pass judgments, without really knowing the inner workings of that family.

In our case, the whole world was looking in—observing, commenting. In his play *Angels in America*, Tony Kushner writes, "The Reagans only speak to each other through their agents." Not completely true, but close enough. There was no way to hide the distance and dissonance in our family, even when we came together for carefully planned photo ops.

The archaeological dig through layers of family history and drama eventually brings most of us to the rawest part of that land—beneath autobiography, beneath recriminations and emotional residue. It brings us to words unsaid, dreams we never shared, questions we kept to ourselves. That's where I ended up. It brought me to this letter. I imagine sometimes talking to both of you now and, Dad, if your faith is accurate and death is just a relocation and not an end, maybe this letter will reach you. My wish is that the idea of a soul, a spirit, still having awareness of a life once lived, is true. You used to tell me about sitting at your own father's funeral when you were thirty years old and suddenly feeling his hand on your earlobe, stroking it as he did when you were a boy. So, perhaps my words will travel across dimensions and reach both of you.

━◀┄►━

MY HOPE IS, ALSO, that this can be a balm of comfort for others as they come to terms with parents and families that have left them searching for answers. Maybe it will provide some comfort. There is a clarifying truth that emerges as we get older: If we don't examine our history and make peace with it, it will become our destiny.

There is another street I visit, not too far away. It's where we lived when it was just the three of us, for the first few years of my life before Ron was born. That house has been torn down too, and replaced by a mansion, but for many years it remained as it was when I was a child. The olive tree that you planted, Dad, right in front, had grown large and full. A few years after you died, Mom got a message from the owner of the house asking if she wanted to visit it, because it was going to be sold and inevitably torn down. I met her there and we walked past the sturdy branches of the olive tree, into the house that echoed with memories.

As we walked down the hallway toward what was once my bedroom, I suddenly remembered sitting on the floor in the hall beside the heating vent, letting warm air envelop me while rain fell hard outside. I remembered my bed in the corner by the window where I would stand up and watch the two of you go out in the evening for dinner. Penny, my nanny, would lean in behind me so I wouldn't topple over. There was a small bar area in the living room; somewhere in my memory I could hear the clinking of ice cubes in cocktail glasses and the tangle of grown-up voices and laughter. At one point, I excused myself from the house tour and went out into the backyard because I felt tears rising up in me. That yard was where I used to play in a sandbox, where I'd sweep back and forth toward an azure sky on a swing set. I didn't know if I actually recalled all of that or if the images were imprinted from photos and home movies. But I did know why I was crying—I think we were happy then in that house, in those years. I don't know why it all changed.

Dad, when you were in your eighties, you said to me, "You've called our family dysfunctional. But we were happy, Patti. Just look at our home movies." I couldn't really accept that home movies and photographs told the story of our family; the tensions and distance had made too much of an impact. Then one day, after you had slipped far away into the uncharted world of Alzheimer's, I pulled out our home movies again. I realized they are part of our story too.

I've watched this footage often, trying to unearth memories of what I'm seeing, but in much of these films I was so young. I have snapshot images, but very few solid memories were formed in those early years. So, like a stranger I study the scenes of 1950s bliss—the happy couple with their new pudgy baby, carrying her around the yard, cooing at her in her stroller. I focus mostly on you, Mom, because Dad was the one operating the Super 8 camera. I look at the warmth in your eyes, I look at how lovingly you hold me and wrap your arms around me. I wish I could remember how your arms felt. By the time complete memories were being formed, I was frightened of you, and it seemed like you had lost the desire to embrace me. You wrote in your memoir that I was a "difficult baby," that I cried and spit up too much, and wanted too much of your attention. But I don't see that irritation and impatience when I look at our home movies. I wonder if those complaints were something you decided on later, after we had turned into our own version of America and Russia, locked in a cold war.

The life we had in the earliest years—the life immortalized in our home movies—was as real as everything that unfolded later. There was love there, and delight; there was laughter and warmth and a mother lifting her toddler up, wiping away her tears when she got scared at being taken into the swimming pool for the first time.

That story about my first swimming lesson was told so often it almost seems like I remember it. As the former lifeguard, Dad, you insisted that your children were never going to drown. So, swimming lessons began early. *Very early.* The story repeated often was that, at first, I got so scared that I kept screaming, "Out, Mommie!" until Mom finally took me out and I ran into her arms, crying. There it is in the home movies—my face crumpling into sobs, Mom's arms around me as she glanced in the direction of the camera manned by you. I don't know how long that particular upheaval lasted, but I was put back in the water and became the water guppy you wanted me to be.

That's the thing about revisiting your childhood—you can travel back with more open eyes, with more room in your heart and your consciousness. You have a chance to see that the story isn't as narrow as you once thought it was. You realize that the whole story of your family is bigger, messier, and often more tender than you once believed. But I still don't know what happened to the tenderness I see in those old movies. Was there ever a way to hold on to it, or was it always going to be fleeting? Our family, like many others, is weighed down by more questions than answers.

As I write this letter, fog billows outside my windows, nestles against the glass. When I was a child, I used to tell you both how much I loved days like this, when we couldn't find the sun to judge the time, and hours seemed to drift by slowly. Dad, you would laugh and say, "You must have lived in England in a past life." I thought about past lives a lot when I was young, not in terms of where I might have lived but who I might have known. I always had a feeling that I had known both of you before. It was a disquieting feeling, a sense that maybe we'd had problems somewhere way back in the folds of time. It was how I tried to make sense of the feeling that you, Mom, always seemed displeased with me. I thought maybe I deserved that displeasure because of some slight from eons ago.

So often, I've thought I had nothing else to say—or write—about our family. After each of your deaths, after eulogizing each of you, I felt like a door was closing, like the dramas and battles we'd lived with were behind me. I felt I could start fresh, look out at smoother vistas and calmer weather as if I didn't have the past that I have. But the truth is, our families are never behind us. They live inside us, sometimes dormant, sometimes raging to be noticed. As we get older, the life we've lived plays out in our minds, our memories; we think about the choices we made, the time we wasted. We start to realize that in so many instances we weren't navigating our own journey, our course had been set by our childhoods, by the decisions we made about our childhoods. In this last third of my life, I have decided to look differently at the life we lived together. As a writer, I have to admit that we are an endlessly interesting family, which is, to be honest, sort of like catnip to a writer.

The spotlight . . .

THE WORLD REMEMBERS YOU not in the ways I do, but in more official terms, as president and first lady. History molds itself around your accomplishments and your public missteps; statues and postage stamps attest to your place in the grand experiment of twentieth-century America. But the world only ever saw us as a family when public events demanded that we be one. Inaugurations brought us together. So did funerals. Especially yours, Dad. Sometimes it seems like only a short time has passed since your death, other times I can feel the weight of the years that have gone by. It was during that time of somber events that we tentatively, almost cautiously, came together as a family. But that relationship, as promising as it seemed for that short week, never had a chance of enduring. We were a house built on sand.

Dad, I know that you loved biblical verses and references. I wonder if you ever lingered on Matthew 7:27, where Jesus spoke about faith, equating it to a wise man building his house on rock, whereas to not have faith was like a foolish man building his house on sand. "And the rain fell, and the floods came," the Bible says, "and the winds blew and beat against that house, and it fell, and great was the fall of it." I wonder if you ever considered that, metaphorically, the idea of a necessary foundation is applicable to many things in life—like a family.

We fell so often it became normal to us. We had no foundational structure beneath us that would allow us to weather even the normal turbulence of life, and certainly not the eddies of a fate that catapulted us into the center ring. The world watched, took note, and never regarded us as a unified family. We did little to change that impression, often speaking on the record to the media in interviews before speaking to one another.

One biblical phrase you used with some frequency, Dad, was "through a glass, darkly." You would say it whenever you wanted to emphasize that many of the mysteries in this life are not meant to be figured out. We will understand everything, you would tell me, on the other side when we go home to God. But here, on this earth, the glass is often dull. As a child, I believed you when you told me that, and I still believe it. Yet, despite that, I long to see this family through a clearer window.

Each of you was mysterious in your own way. The bright light of the world glaring down ironically made you both more opaque, more mysterious. As the light shone brighter, the shadows got deeper. Words and stories were always how I navigated my way through shadows. They served as my beacon.

When I was small, I went to a preschool with a wide flagstone driveway and a huge green field beside the house that served as the school. Mom, you used to pick me up there and you once said you always knew where to find me—not playing with the other kids, but in a far corner of the grassy field, my face buried in a book, taking refuge in stories that were not my own. You once said you knew way back then that I would be a writer. The thing about writers is that we can't bypass a good story, and we can't let go of one once we've started taking it apart and looking at all the inside components. Some of us are either lucky or cursed to have those good stories in our own lives.

When I walked up to the podium to deliver your eulogy, twelve years after Dad's death, I remember taking a long deep breath, thinking, Here I am again letting the world into the war-torn landscape of the Reagan family. But it was different on that day—a day of storm, with rain clouds gathering in the sky and the wind turning cold. I'd worked hard on your eulogy because I'd worked hard on looking at our relationship differently. I'd forced myself to look past the angry times, the cold silences that could last for months, even the fear that always sat inside me whenever I was near you. I had searched and foraged, and I had found moments when there was just love there. Memory is a funny thing—we tend to remember the bad times more clearly than the good, but the good memories sit there patiently, waiting for us to find them.

As soon as your doctor said you didn't have much time left, maybe a week or so, I began working on your eulogy, spending hours on it as the light changed outside and evening brushed across the sky. I felt that you deserved that time. I felt we both deserved it. We had pursued many long roads into war, but there were patches of peace too, and I wanted to honor those, even the ones that seemed small. Like the day I was playing at a friend's house—I was probably seven or eight—and I fell onto the fireplace hearth, cracking my head open. My friend's parents called you and you rushed to get me, gently helping me into the car, talking soothingly to me, even holding out your hand to catch my vomit when I got sick. I remember that car ride—the blood coming from my head wound, the nausea, the dizziness, but what I also remember is the certainty that you loved me and wanted to take care of me.

There is an artistry to memory. Some people take blunt tools to it, pound it into the shape they have decided upon. Others treat it like tapestry, weaving threads, snipping some off, tying careful knots at certain places. I've reflected a lot on how the two of you treated the memories of your past. You each had your own techniques for re-shaping your childhoods, your early adulthoods. Dad, you were the weaver of stories, describing details that made the listener feel as if they were there, traveling back in time with you. I've no doubt that there was embellishment, but I always felt the core of each story was truthful. What I learned over the years is that you took memories you didn't want to visit and plunged them into darkness, choosing oblivion for what you didn't know how to handle. Mom, when it came to your past, you wielded an anvil and a sledgehammer. Your own version of events was what you decided upon, and heaven help the poor fool who disagreed with you. I remember in the 1980 presidential campaign, Mike Deaver, who worked on Dad's campaign and would go on to be chief of staff, telling you that you shouldn't have gotten angry at a reporter who referred to Loyal Davis as your stepfather when he was, in fact, your stepfather, not your birth father. I believe you turned Mike Deaver into a pillar of salt with the look you gave him; it's nothing short of miraculous that he recovered.

In my eulogy for you, I spoke about a memory that has stayed with me for decades. I was a teenager, it was summer, and we had rented a beach house north of Malibu for a couple of weeks, as we usually did. One evening, as a vivid sunset streaked across the sky, I looked out and saw the two of you sitting on the sand close together, your heads tilted in conversation. There was so much vastness around you—the blue Pacific, the orange sky, miles of white sand—and then there was the circle of your own private world, as clear as if it had been traced around you. Indestructible, impenetrable, an island for two. That evening I knew, as night drifted in and the light changed, I would carry that image with me for the rest of my life. And I have.

That circle of just the two of you was the overriding reality of our family. It dominated everything. Many years later I told someone that, as children, we had the sense that if we were spirited away by pirates, you and Dad would miss us . . . but you'd be fine. I said it lightly, with humor, but it was because of that impenetrable circle that we were a family with no real foundation.

When I think of you, Dad, the images that come to me are not of the president in the Oval Office, or the man standing in front of Congress and the nation giving a State of the Union address, or the leader of the free world greeting Mikhail Gorbachev. I think of you as the swimmer who fell in love with the river when you were a boy. "It was wide as the town and twice as long," you used to say. The Rock River ran through your childhood as the place to swim in summer and skate on in winter. I think of you as the lifeguard who plunged into the currents and saved seventy-seven people, something you were proud of all your life.

I see you also as the horseman who said, "There's nothing as good for the inside of a man as the outside of a horse." You could calm a skittish horse, sail over jumps as if you'd ridden all your life, which you hadn't. You could issue clipped commands in a soft but stern voice when you were riding, and the horse would willingly obey. To watch you sail over jumps was to stand in awe of the exquisite bond between man and animal. In teaching me how to ride, you also taught me to get back on after I fell off. "You never want to let fear get the best of you," you'd say.

When I was a child, you were constantly teaching me things, preparing me with your implacable confidence for what might come my way. You took me out into the ocean and taught me about catching waves, told me how to slip down the back of a wave if it was just about to break, or dive down to the still waters beneath if it had already broken, a lesson I can also see now in metaphorical terms. You counseled me on how to ignore a bully, after I faked being sick because a boy at school was tormenting me. You had a plan if there was an earthquake, or a fire. But the one thing you couldn't prepare me for was the direction your life would take. I've often wondered if you knew, in the secret caverns of your heart, that you wanted to lead this country. That your dreams were big and endless and couldn't be contained. America was always a topic of conversation, even when I was small. As the years mounted, I came to feel that America was a presence, an entity, who was sitting at the dinner table with us and getting most of the attention. Eventually, I must confess, I developed a bad case of sibling rivalry with this country.

It wasn't until you got Alzheimer's that I came to appreciate America's companionship. People approached me with compassion, with sympathy. They shared stories about their own experiences with a loved one who had dementia. Overnight, we became the poster family for Alzheimer's. And overnight, I found that it was comforting to have everyone know the diagnosis that was steering you to the end of your life. I noticed the transformation in myself, the middle-aged daughter taking on responsibilities that I couldn't have imagined a decade earlier. I could sense the support and concern of strangers, which kept me afloat. We were in a realm beyond politics; there was no way that everyone who spoke to me agreed with your politics. They were responding to you as a human being, not just as a political figure, and there was sustenance in that.

I wonder now how you would feel about where

America has come to. Maybe you occasionally look in from beyond—I often allow myself to imagine that—and when I do, I see you, the lifeguard who spent summers rescuing people, with tears in your eyes. The tears of a leader who loved the country he was elected to serve. The presidency you so revered has been sullied by a man incapable of truth or empathy. A man who refused to attend the inauguration of the next president and stirred up a riot in the nation's Capitol, gleefully watching it on television rather than trying to stop it. There have been neo-Nazis parading through American cities, the vilification of anyone who isn't white, the blatant murder of Black people, too often by police. And the mass shootings. Theaters, concerts, nightclubs, supermarkets, churches, and schools—small children mowed down with semiautomatic weapons. And, even more unimaginable, small children bringing guns to school. If you are looking in, you must be heavy with grief. You must be thinking, What has happened to the America I loved?

That America was still thriving when you died. People eight rows deep crowded along streets and on freeway overpasses as we drove by in the motorcade, your heavy coffin in the hearse. Grief brought people together, made walls between them tumble down. Tears softened those walls and bonded people together with fondness for a good man, regardless of whether or not they agreed with him. We aren't that country anymore. Now there seems to just be rage, incinerating the dream of what America was supposed to be.

When you were recovering from the bullets that John Hinckley fired into you, you said, "They told me he fired devastator bullets. Those bullets are meant to fragment, to cause maximum damage. I never even knew they existed." Your blue eyes were wide and puzzled, and I thought I saw a tinge of fear in them. What would you think of the AR-15s, now brazenly legal, that are being used to slaughter innocent people—young schoolchildren, concertgoers, shoppers—in a matter of seconds? What would you think of the reluctance to ban them? Of eighteen-year-olds with histories of emotional instability being allowed to buy them? America has turned into a killing field and the elected officials who are entrusted with our safety are doing little to change that. Grief has become pervasive in America right now.

In your farewell speech to the nation as a soon-to-be-former president, you said, "Man is not free unless government is limited." We are now in a time when the government is essentially taking ownership of women's bodies, a time when free and fair elections have been threatened by officials who should be protecting them. We are living in a time when democracy is gradually unraveling, and autocracy is leaning in hard. You also said in that speech, "Freedom is fragile." Millions of us are feeling that fragility these days. You spoke of informed patriotism. But with the press under attack, with a former president and his supporters calling the free press "the enemy of the people," informed patriotism might just be a pipe dream.

Perhaps, if you are looking down here, you know that, after years of resenting America for claiming so much of you, I too have come to love this country. And I am heartbroken over what it is descending into. One of the gifts you gave me was the ability to feel this heartbreak.

There are times when I wake up in the dead of night and imagine telling you that.

I've long felt, Dad, that part of the reason you were driven to succeed is because your own father stumbled into failure again and again. Many people have said that you wouldn't have achieved the heights you did without Mom, that she was responsible for your success. I disagree. You were determined not to be your father. Jack Reagan's drinking defined so much of your early life—the nights he didn't come home because he was passed out in a bar, or the nights he did and careened into your mother's disapproval. On one occasion, she gathered you and your brother and was planning to leave him, but practicality thwarted her plan—she had nowhere to go. Jack drank up the money your family needed; he drank up opportunities and jobs and he embarrassed you, although you never would have admitted that.

There was a story you told that was, at its root, a story of humiliation and fear. You were eleven years old, coming home from playing basketball at the Y on an ice-cold night in February. You expected your house to be empty, but when you came up the walkway there was your father, Jack, sprawled in the snow, passed-out drunk. His hair was caked with snow, the smell of whiskey drifted off him into the white air. You stood over him for a moment, tempted to just go inside and pretend he wasn't there. But you knew neighbors were probably looking out their windows, and you also knew he could freeze to death out there. You grabbed fistfuls of his overcoat and dragged him inside to his bed. I heard you tell the story a few times over the years and once I asked you if that was the only time you found him like that. I've always suspected it wasn't. You never answered me. You just said that alcoholism is a disease, and it wasn't his fault. So,

I'm left to wonder, how many other times did you find your father laid out drunk? How many times did you help him and then decide to forget that it happened?

One of the reasons I've often thought about that story is that it played at the edges of the often tearful resentment I felt over you not being a more attentive father. At some point, I had to look more clearly at your life and ask myself, Where would he have learned how to be an available and attentive father? Not from Jack. In the decade of your Alzheimer's, I knew with absolute clarity that I had to grow up. Part of growing up was learning to see you through adult eyes as you retreated to times long gone, to different stages of who you once were. I saw you young, insecure, the nearsighted kid who sat beside his mother as she read to him, and who learned to read himself by the age of five. I saw you as the swaggering teen, and as the young actor who willed himself to have confidence because he was so determined to succeed. I saw you alone but never lonely. And I saw what I had always suspected— you were so at home in your relationship to God, your silent conversations with Him, in many ways you needed no one else. You learned that reverence, that trust in God, from your mother Nelle. I remember she was tiny, with kind eyes, and hands that reached for me. But my memories of her are faint and scattered; she died too soon for me to get to know her. It's a sorrow that sits in the center of my life. I think she would have anchored me in the same ways she anchored you.

So much of my earlier life was defined by a longing for your attention and your approval, followed by the inevitable disappointment and even anger when I knew I was never going to get either. When I was finally willing to look at that head-on, I could see past the emotions and understand all the ways that the terrain of our lives is carved up and fenced off by the way our parents chose to parent us. We try to separate ourselves from them, compose an identity that has nothing to do with them, but that never works out very well. It's like sawing off an arm and then trying to climb up a rope.

I heard Rosanne Cash tell a story about something that happened with her father, Johnny Cash. He was performing at Carnegie Hall and Rosanne was going to go to the show. In his hotel room before heading to the venue he asked her if she would come onstage with him and sing "I Still Miss Someone." Rosanne says she was harboring some resentment over perceived childhood wounds, which she later couldn't even remember, and she declined. Her father said okay, and turned away. Then came one of those epiphanous moments that usher in profound change. The look of his back struck her—how many times she had seen him like that when he was in the spotlight and she was standing in the wings. She said, "Dad, I changed my mind. I'll do it." They sang the duet together that night and she says it was a profound moment—to feel something healed as they shared the spotlight together.

Our parents are part of us—the sweet moments, the difficult memories. All of it. We find ourselves when we accept that.

Dad, once you stepped into the world of politics, your life was immersed in it. These days, I allow myself to be open to the weightiness of your legacy, finally accepting that you are part of who I am. I am the daughter of a man who, for eight years, parented America. Often the biblical phrase "sins of the father" intrudes on me, since many people choose to come after me for what they consider your derelictions, even your sins.

You would probably be amused that, after my public rebellion against your policies, I have occasionally taken on the task of trying to explain a few of your positions—not to excuse or endorse, but simply to shed light on how I feel you arrived at some of them. Like abortion. I've peeled away the layers of rigid disagreement that always weighed us down, looking for the stories underneath. When you were governor of California and an abortion bill was on your desk, you wrote and spoke of your soul-searching, the hours you spent in contemplation over a woman's intimate decision to end her pregnancy. You ended up signing a bill that, for the first time, allowed abortions for rape, incest, and dangers to the mother's physical or mental health.

I've thought about this so often—how, with the exception of those situations, you didn't believe abortion should be a right—and I feel that the loss of your two-day-old daughter—the loss you and Jane Wyman went through toward the end of your marriage—had a huge influence on you. The language used by the anti-abortion movement—killing an unborn child, murdering a fetus—must have, I assume, tumbled right into the grief you never talked about and possibly never even acknowledged.

You never talked about that child at all. I now know her name was Christine. I didn't learn about her until I was in my forties. A loss like that—the death of a newborn so briefly in this world—carves out a wound deep inside. And if grief is pushed away, if the heart isn't allowed to fracture and break, the wound gets deeper, sodden with all the tears that haven't been cried. Grief can be sidelined for a while, but it can't be banished. Maybe your silence about Christine was because she was a part of your life before Mom. We were never supposed to talk about Jane or your history with her, and Christine was part of that history—the shadow child who died so soon after being born. Somewhere along the line, I assume you and Mom decided to keep that entire part of your life behind a veil.

I never knew about Michael and Maureen, my half siblings, until I was eight years old and Michael came to live with us. Ron was two, still a toddler in a high chair, and when you told me I had an older half brother—emphasis on *half*—I was excited that I'd have someone to play with, talk to. I was a lonely child—shy, nearsighted, and insecure around other people. Our house was rather stiff and strict, but I suddenly imagined things transforming, becoming more fun with the arrival of a fourteen-year-old boy whom I'd just been told was my brother. (I did not take note of the half part.) At that time, a tall blond woman used to come to the house occasionally and sit in the den talking with Mom. They spoke in low voices, it all seemed very adult. I only knew her as Maureen. One day, shortly before Michael's arrival, she was leaving after visiting for a while, and I excitedly told her that I had another brother—an older brother! She bent down, got close to my face, and said, "Well, don't you know who I am? I'm your sister."

The memory is seared into me. I remember how the afternoon sun slanted across the black slate floor. I remember how Maureen had her purse looped over her arm and how her lipstick was perfectly applied. And I remember something breaking in me. Suddenly discovering a new sibling wasn't fun anymore. The world had become unpredictable. How many other brothers and sisters did I have? Would a new one arrive every week? Every month? With the drama of an eight-year-old, I ran into my bedroom and threw myself down on my bed to cry. What I also remember is that no one came in to talk to me, so I returned to the cocoon of aloneness that I had gotten used to.

If this were a movie scene (I know how much you like those), we would cut to roughly thirty-five years later when your biographer, Edmund Morris, told me who he was dedicating the book to.

"I'm going to dedicate it to Christine Reagan," he said on a drizzly day in New York, where I was then living. We had met for coffee.

"Who's that?" I asked incredulously. Another unknown family member? I was eight years old again, wondering how many other Reagan siblings would surface.

Edmund told me the story of Christine, the tiny two-day-old baby who died just about the time that your marriage to Jane Wyman was in its death throes. You had gotten pneumonia filming a movie with Shirley Temple and were confined to a hospital bed; at one point you were near death yourself. So you couldn't visit Christine during her short stay on this earth. You never got to say goodbye. I think now that the distance imposed by circumstance helped shape your views later about abortion. There was a child you never saw, never touched, a child who died out of reach. Michael told me recently that Jane never forgot about Christine. I don't believe you did either; you just willed her memory away, pushing it into the blackness of oblivion, a place already crowded with things you didn't want to look at.

I've sometimes asked myself why I feel so compelled now to try to explain what was behind some of your positions, some of your language. I'm an unlikely person to take on the task of trying to explain you and even at times defend you. There is often such a wide chasm between you as a public figure, an elected leader, and the man whose hand I reached for as a child and in whose eyes I found comfort, that perhaps I'm trying to reconcile those two men.

I want people to see the father who took me up the hill in back of our house to fly kites on days when the wind was strong. On one of those days, with white clouds scudding across the afternoon sky, I asked you why people come in different colors. We were both wearing jackets on that chilly day, and our feet kicked up small clouds of dust as we headed for the hilltop where you would let the kite out until it danced on wind currents. You slowed your pace and told me that God made all His creations in different colors. The horses at our ranch were different colors; our dog Lucky, a black-and-white collie, was different from other dogs. But you told me that makes no difference to God. They are all His children, just like people who also come in different colors. They are no different in God's eyes.

I want people to know the story about when you were in college, on the football team, and the team was playing near your hometown of Dixon, Illinois. When you all got to the hotel, the two Black players on your team were forbidden to enter. You said you wouldn't stay there either and you took them to your parents' house for the night. Your father had raised you to abhor racism; he forbade you to see the 1915 film *Birth of a Nation*, the three-hour D. W. Griffith homage to racist propaganda, which had the Ku Klux Klan riding in at the end to save the South from Blacks. Your mother was devout in her religious beliefs and never looked down on anyone; to her, everyone was a child of God.

I want people to know that when you were governor of California, a local country club gifted you a membership which you refused because that particular club wouldn't allow Jews to apply for membership.

I want it known that when I was about nine years old you ran a film for me that you warned me would be upsetting. But, you said it was important that I know what had happened in the world—and what must never happen again. It was the George Stevens film of American troops going into Dachau at the end of World War II, encountering piles of bodies and the barely alive survivors who were skeletal and broken, who had endured unimaginable horrors. Mom had a friend who was a Holocaust survivor, and I had asked innocently what the tattooed numbers were on her arm; that's what led to you showing me that film. You talked to me afterward—about the evil that humans are capable of, and the importance of looking hard at history to ensure such horrors will never happen again. It's been decades since I saw that film and it still plays in my mind as if I watched it yesterday.

I want people to remember that in 1982, you read a newspaper story in the morning about a Black family—the Butlers—in College Park Woods, Maryland, who had won a civil suit against a Ku Klux Klan leader for burning a cross on their lawn five years earlier. That burning cross was what finally propelled them to act after several prior incidents. The Klan had first driven a car into their lamppost and on another occasion had dumped garbage on their front lawn. The Butlers were one of several Black families who had moved into the area, and they had become targets of the Klan. After reading the newspaper story, Dad, you said you wanted to go visit them that day, so after all your meetings wrapped up late in the afternoon, you and Mom boarded Marine One and flew to College Park Woods. It was a balmy May day, and the two of you sat in the Butlers' home visiting with them for almost an hour. You told them, in reference to the cross-burning, "This should never happen in America." Mom hugged Mrs. Butler goodbye when the two of you left, and you, Dad, shook Mr. Butler's hand. You'd brought them a jar of jelly beans. The Butlers spoke to the press afterward and said they felt there was nothing political in the visit, that it was sincere and heartfelt.

Moments like that stand in stark contrast to an

agenda of cutting programs that had been designed
to help poor families, most of whom were minorities. One of the unanswered questions that I will
have to live with is how those two things could
coexist—the man who raised me to look at all people as God's children, who didn't hesitate to visit
and comfort a Black family after they had been targeted because of their race . . . and the government
policies under your watch that ended up harming
minorities in this country.

Many years ago, I read a book by Aldous Huxley called *The Art of Seeing*. He touched on a theory
about the psychology of vision abnormalities, like
nearsightedness and farsightedness. He suggested
that the nearsighted person needs to bring things
close in order to see them clearly—both physically,
because of faulty vision, but also psychologically.
There is some fear, some uncertainty to stretching
oneself. So things that are far away, out in the distance, are kept out of focus, hard to see; they need
to be pulled close, where it's safer, in order to be
fully recognized. Psychologically, emotionally, the
person is unwilling to extend themselves outward
enough to fully grasp what's far away from them.
Your nearsightedness defined so much of your life.
You were the young boy in his bedroom with his
face buried in a book; to look beyond that book

meant uncertainty because everything was blurry. Although in that blur was your alcoholic father who made your family's life undependable and insecure. There were good reasons to stay buried in books. Then one day you picked up your father's glasses and put them on. You spoke about the world suddenly coming into focus. You saw a butterfly in all its fragile beauty. But your poor vision determined things in your later life. You wanted to join the military but couldn't because you failed the eye exam, even though you squinted and tried to cheat. I wonder, if you had read Huxley's book, would you have seen yourself in the parallels he drew between physical nearsightedness and psychological myopia?

Before the world moved in . . .

Dad, when I search for you, I find you in the green world of open fields and long rides on horseback, in the cresting and breaking of ocean waves, blue distance between us as you beckoned me to swim out to you, and always in your stories about the river. It was a more innocent time; I guess I thought it would always be like that. I wasn't prepared for it to end.

So, to recapture what we once had, I spin back through time to Saturdays at our ranch, inland from Malibu. All week I looked forward to Saturday; I rehearsed in my head what I would discuss with you when we went on our horseback rides together. Mom didn't really enjoy riding, she stayed back at the ranch house, collecting eggs from the chickens, picking fruit from the plum tree during the summer. Ron was six years younger than me, not big enough for riding yet, so this was my time alone with you. I drank in every moment of it—brushing the horses, cleaning their hooves, watching you hoist the saddle first onto my horse, then onto yours. Before I got tall enough to mount the horse myself, you helped me up, checked the girth to make sure it was tight enough. And then, with the sound of hooves marking our departure, the land opened up in front of us.

It was deep green in winter, bursting with wildflowers in spring. I remember the sight of your back as you rode in front of me on a narrow trail through the oak grove, sunlight and shadow dancing across you, an out-of-reach chiaroscuro. I talked to you about my history teacher, who was extremely fond of Abraham Lincoln, and I complained about math, which I hated. I talked to you about God, which had been a common topic between us since I was small. I told you my dream in which I met Jesus on the beach on a moonlit night. What I never told you was that in my dream I talked to Jesus about how sad I was much of the time, how I felt like I didn't fit in anywhere. I don't know why I kept that from you; maybe I thought you would assume I was blaming you and Mom, or maybe I just felt embarrassed. You pointed out plants that should be avoided, like poison ivy, or thistle which would blister your skin. You told me that rattlesnakes are God's creatures too, and it's only okay to kill one if it is an immediate threat. Rattlesnakes can only strike if they are coiled, and then they can only reach half their length. To calculate their age, count the rattles. I memorized everything you told me.

My favorite ride was when we meandered down the wide trail that bisected the main part of the ranch and went into a field where you and Ray, our ranch hand, had built jumps from old phone poles. You taught me to sail over them, directing me toward the lower jumps and coaching me on my form, on how to give my horse his head while still maintaining control. My horse, Quicksilver, was an early-retired racehorse who had suffered an injury; you bought him and presented him to me as a birthday present. Just past the field was a sloping hill; we would canter up to the top and look down on the neighboring ranch. The land below us looked like the most peaceful oasis I'd ever seen.

Trees arched over a pond, spilled shade across pas-
tures and gullies that seemed impossibly green. It
looked like a painting.

One day, on a hot summer afternoon when the
land had turned brown and gold, Quicksilver got
spooked on our way home. He bolted and I fell off.
I wasn't hurt, but I was scared to get back on him
and I told you that I was just going to hold his bri-
dle and walk him back to the barn. You wouldn't let
me. You said that since I wasn't hurt, I needed to
get back on and keep riding, that way I would get
over my fear and my horse would sense that I wasn't
scared. "You always get back on after you fall," you
said. I knew I was being given a lesson about more
than riding, and I often return to that day—to
the dust and the heat and the grip of fear, to the
instruction of your voice—I return to it when life
throws me to the ground and I need to get back up.

I learned so much on those acres of land. You
explained to me the cycle of life in nature—that
death is part of it. An animal dies and another feeds
off it. The first vultures I ever saw were feeding on
a dead rabbit. I started crying, but you quelled my
tears by telling me that everything dies eventually.
It was that rabbit's time to go, and the vultures
would live by eating it. You told me vultures never
attack any living creature; they patiently wait for

something to die so they can eat. You said God created nature with perfect balance.

But one summer day, when I drove out alone
with you to the ranch, nature did not seem to be in
perfect balance. Nancy D, your beloved horse with
whom you had an unbreakable bond, was in foal
and had been put into one of the stalls because her
time to deliver was near. When we drove into the
barnyard, Ray, who lived at the ranch and cared for
it, met us at the car with tears streaking his face.
We quickly got out and stood under the canopy of
eucalyptus trees as he told us that Nancy D had
died suddenly during the night. She'd had some
kind of virus or infection that was undetectable
despite all the vet's visits, and it suddenly killed her
and the colt she was carrying. I immediately started
crying, but when I looked at you, your face was
tilted upward to the sky; your eyes had a faraway,
almost prayerful look to them, and your expression
was loving and warm, not disfigured by tears.

"Why aren't you crying?" I asked you through
my own tears.

You glanced down at me briefly and then
returned your gaze to the heavens. "Because I'm
thinking of all the beautiful years I had with her."

I so wish I could talk to you now as my sixteen-
year-old pug nears the end of her life. I've had Gra-

cie since she was a tiny puppy, we've been through so much together, and there are times when grief already drives me to my knees because I know what's coming. What I learned from you that day was the importance of gratitude, of grabbing on to the richness of time spent together, even though I'm certain you grieved deeply as well. But somehow you knew how to find a balance between grief and gratitude, between tears and the treasures of two lives intertwined. It's moments like that—the summer day warm and lazy around us, the paintbrush sky, the pungent smell of eucalyptus trees, and your eyes reaching up to heaven—that make me long for you. In those memories, the world that claimed so much of you falls away and we are just father and daughter, the river of life carrying us with no promise that any of it will make sense.

Those Saturday ranch days had a predictable ending. We'd drive back home to Pacific Palisades in the late afternoon, and we would always stop at a Frosties stand along the Coast Highway. We'd all get vanilla Frosties and eat them on the way home, trying not to spill them in the car. One day, Dad, you went up to the window with me to order and the woman was very snippy to you. You didn't let it ruffle you; you were kind and polite to her, and as we went back to the car with our Frosties, I asked you why you were so nice to her when she'd been rude to you.

"You never know what someone is going through in their life," you told me. "She could have just gotten really bad news—maybe she's sick with something, or maybe a family member died. You just never know, so it's better to be kind."

I try to remember that in my daily life, but I doubt I will ever be as successful at it as you were.

Our ranch trips were one of the most dependable things we did as a family. We never did what other families usually did—go to amusement parks or movies together. You and Mom had friends who would take me, and later Ron, to all these places. They were always couples who didn't have children of their own, so they were sort of surrogate parents to us, at least for a day. One of those couples always had me spend the night before we went to Disneyland early the next morning. Their house was all white inside—the carpet, the furniture. I remember being scared that I would get a smudge of food or dirt on some part of their carefully manicured decor. At some point in school, listening to the other kids, I realized that the way we did things was not typical. Other families piled into the car and headed out to amusement parks and other adventures, but we never did. I asked you once, Mom, why you and

Dad never took us to any of these places. You told me that when I was quite young, the two of you had taken me to Disneyland. We were on the tea-cup ride—the ride where several people sit in giant teacups and then whir around the tracks, bumping into other teacups and spinning around in tight circles. According to you, people recognized Dad, since he was on television every week on *General Electric Theater*, and a crowd swarmed us, making it impossible for us to enjoy ourselves.

The funny thing about that is, I remember the teacup ride. It's one of those snapshot memories from early childhood that's frozen in time, imprinted with specific details. I'm guessing I must have been four, maybe five. Disneyland opened in 1955, and Ron wasn't born yet. Our family was still just the three of us, sitting close together in a moving teacup. I remember it was a crisp day and I had a sweater on. I remember feeling dizzy from the teacups swirling around and I didn't like it when we bumped into other teacups, which is supposed to be the fun part. What I don't recall is a crowd of people descending on us. So, I don't really know why you and Dad delegated childhood outings to other people, and when I ponder it now, it seems sad. It falls into the empty well of memories we don't have.

There were scents to my childhood that, when I

encounter them now, send me reeling back. There are still some honeysuckle vines in our old neighborhood. I passed by some on one of my walks, breathed them in, and was again that small girl walking with our nanny Myra as she pushed the stroller that held my new baby brother. Myra had a thick Scottish brogue; she was slender, with dark hair and glasses, and was always patient. I remember finding out at some point that, on her time off, she would go to a neighbor's house to swim in the pool because she was afraid to ask you, Mom, if she could swim in ours.

In winter there was the smell of rain and wet earth, woodsmoke from fireplaces. When we drove out to the ranch on Saturdays the smell of the ocean filled the car; often damp billows of fog drifted over us. Then we turned inland into the smell of oak, eucalyptus, and wild grasses. Miles of land ribboned out around us. I polish the sweeter memories as if they are gems that need to be cared for so light can shine through. But so much of my feeling about home is shadowy, murky with history.

I don't remember ever walking into our home with a sense of security and a feeling that I belonged. Crossing the threshold always made me nervous, as if I weren't sure I should be there. From a young age I was attracted to stories about wanderers and pilgrims—people traveling across the land alone, with nothing but the possessions they carried. When the Bel Air Fire was looming near our home and the two of you sat up all night with the cars packed, ready to evacuate, I remember looking around my room, with the floral wallpaper and matching bedspread, with two porcelain dolls high up on the shelves—dolls that had been given as Christmas gifts, which I wasn't supposed to play with. I realized there was nothing in that room I needed to take. Nothing there, or in the rest of the house, felt like home to me. I went out to the kitchen and poured dog food into a bag, made sure Lucky's leash was nearby, but that was my only preparation for an evacuation that ended up not being necessary.

It wasn't just me who noticed the stiffness, the absence of warmth and inclusion. Many years later, Maureen would say to me that whenever she visited, she was never offered something to eat or drink, and there was always an awkwardness about coming in and sitting down somewhere, as if no one knew where to put her (her words, not mine).

I've thought of this often over the years because the whole concept of home has been a problem for me. I've moved often in my life, never quite feeling I belonged, and after I finally bought a home in

Los Angeles in my thirties, I ended up making the most disastrous decision of my life. After getting into, and out of, an abusive relationship, I sold my house at the bottom of the market, lost pretty much everything, and fled across the country to the East Coast. I didn't understand at the time that wanting to run away was part of an old playbook and creating a home—keeping a home—was deep work that I desperately needed to do. It was a mistake that reverberated throughout my life for decades because from that point on I was always in some sort of financial difficulty and rootlessness became normal for me. Only now—more than thirty years later—have I finally been able to buy a home, but I know that ghosts are never completely silent. Who I was as a child, poised to run away at a moment's notice, can still tug on me, telling me that I don't really deserve a home.

Here is what I wonder now, Mom: Was the home you created for us a replica of the home you lived in as a very young child, the one you never talked about? When your mother left you with her relatives and took off down the road, did you find yourself in a home that was not warm and welcoming, an environment that never wrapped itself around you protectively? Was it a home where you always felt like an outsider? Your history was so edited and redacted there was never a chance for me to know the answer, but we do tend to re-create things in life that we have never come to terms with. The past tumbles ahead into the future if we don't step into the road and stop it.

I know for you, Dad, ours was not the type of home you grew up in. The story of when your college football team had an away game near Dixon and the two Black players were not allowed into the hotel was something you told in an interview once. You described taking them back to your parents' house, where all of you spent the night, and the interviewer asked if you had any trepidations about just showing up at your parents' house with two of your teammates.

"No," you said emphatically. "I knew my parents. I knew my home. Of course it would be fine."

I wonder if you ever noticed how markedly different our home was from the home your parents created. Did you ever sense the awkwardness, the stiffness? Or was that something you pushed away into the distance, into the mist of things you didn't want to see? Ironically, you actually had a number of homes when you were growing up. Jack went from job to job because of his drinking, which meant that all of you were forced to move quite often. You said once that you were always the new kid in school. Yet when you described the environment in any of those homes, it was still dependably loving and inclusive.

I look back down the years at my childhood as if I'm going back in time to an ancient place. Seasons rolled by predictably in those years. Spring coaxed wildflowers and sheaths of green grasses from the earth. I used to sit on a hillside at our ranch, hypnotized by the long grasses rippling on the fields below me. I felt close to God in those times, awestruck by the beauty of the world He'd created. We had winters when rain fell for days on end. There were thunderstorms that lasted half the night. When Ron was a toddler, you and Mom would bring us into your bed, along with Lucky, who would nestle at our feet. We'd all lie there together watching flashes of lightning illuminate the dark room and then wait for the claps of thunder—at first so close we put our hands over our ears, but then eventually getting softer as the storm moved away. Ron would flap his hands and cry out, "It's going to blow my whiskers off!" The two of you loved that, so he kept saying it.

It's been so long since we've had winters like that. Now the earth is sweltering, drying up, choking on all the poisons we've sent into the atmosphere. I wonder how you would feel, Dad, about a planet turning to ash and dust. We are burning down our home, and no one is doing enough to stop it. Storms are leveling entire towns and swaths of cities. It feels biblical, earth's revenge over what we have done to her. You used to talk to me about Jesus's return to earth. You would say that the Second Coming would occur when the world was at the tipping point for disaster. Here is what I never told you—I'd lie awake at night thinking about that with a feeling, a premonition really, roiling in me that this would happen in my lifetime. I wasn't completely certain about Jesus returning, but I had the overwhelming sense that I was here on this earth to witness its last days. I think of that often now because it feels like my premonition was accurate.

We are always the children we once were. Years mold us, transform us, but deep inside a child lingers and asks to be understood. If we are lucky, someone left us with a record of our childhood—home movies or photographs, images that stir up memories, that remind us of younger times and allow us to look at our parents through grown-up eyes. I've looked at so many old photos of the two of you when you were dating, and of Christmases in our first house, which I don't have many clear memories of. But it's our home movies I've studied the most, looking for insights, for markers along the trail that will better help me figure out a family that wasn't very good at being one.

I watch the silent film footage of the two of you starting your life together, of my earliest days after the first wail of being born. You were a shiny Hollywood couple whose happiness with each other radiated. I watch, hoping to find clues that I missed before. It's so much harder to write to you, Mom—I still fight through traces of bitterness and wrestle with the complexity of our relationship. When did things turn dark between us? Was it gradual, or was there a break, like a lightning bolt shattering what we'd had when I was small and pouty and dressed in baby clothes? I don't know the answer, but something in me keeps wanting to look for one, as if having a map will make everything more understandable.

I prefer to linger for a while in the innocent times when it was just the three of us in the house on Amalfi Drive. The house with turquoise appliances in the kitchen, the olive tree out front, and a backyard with rosebushes and a sandbox where I played for long stretches of time. I watch your face in these films, Mom, as you hold me up and encourage me to wave at Dad and his ever-present camera. I look now not only at your smile but at your eyes—infused with love and happiness, not only when you turn to Dad but when you turn to me. When you rush to scoop me up as I crawl toward the edge of the raised patio, as you shower me with kisses, laughing into the sunlight. I study your expression as you turn your face toward mine. But the eyes I see in our home movies aren't the eyes I remember. So, I need to memorize them, tell myself that all the maternal feelings one expects from a mother were once there, preserved in the luster of those young days. I remember the hallway in that house, and how it felt to pad along the wood floor between our bedrooms. In my room, my bed was by a window that faced the driveway and the street. I remember sometimes crying as I watched you and Dad get in the car and go out for dinner. Nothing that my nanny, the very British Penny, said could soothe me. I have a faint recollection of being frightened that perhaps you were leaving for good, that you might not come back to me. I wonder now if I had some seedling of an instinct that your and Dad's relationship functioned in its own universe. Maybe even as a toddler I sensed that I would always be an outsider, that in one way or another, you would always be leaving.

Yet in those early home movies and photographs, the evidence is, Mom, that you welcomed

the mosaic landscape of motherhood and got enjoy-
ment from it. It also seemed like our home was
more lively, more filled with extended family and
close friends, than it would be in later years. Dad,
your mother Nelle was there for Christmases. And
Mom, your stepbrother and his wife were there
with their son, Barton, who was only a bit older
than me. The story is that his name was one of the
first words I learned to say. The photographs show a
warm home, filled with family. But as years passed,
that wasn't the home I would come to remember.
I wouldn't see Barton again for decades—not until
the 1981 presidential inauguration. We hardly
ever saw my aunt and uncle. Nelle developed what
was then called senility and was placed in a home,
which I remember visiting once—pale green walls,
elderly people in cots, and the distinct smells of
urine and age. My godfather William Holden was
also at our Amalfi house, tan and smiling, holding
a drink and a cigarette as he lounged in an armchair. I would never see him again until I was in my
thirties and I ran into him at a restaurant. Before
that, he was a man in framed photographs dis-
played on shelves. He was the handsome actor in
movies I saw on television, and someone you spoke
about, Dad, as a friend from long ago.

I never told either of you about running into

him. It was 1981, we weren't talking much then because of my political activism. I was out to dinner with a few friends at a Beverly Hills restaurant, my Secret Service agents trying to be discreet at a nearby table. Suddenly I looked across the restaurant and saw William Holden sitting with a couple of people. In something reminiscent of a movie scene, he turned at that same moment, saw me, and we both stood up and walked toward each other. We embraced, and I said to him, "I've missed you in my life." He said he'd missed me too and gave me his phone number, telling me to please call and we'd get together. I still don't know why I didn't call immediately. Why didn't I try to reach him the next day? A couple of weeks went by, I was *intending* to call, and then I read the news of his death, and the devastating details. Alone in his condo, extremely intoxicated, he slipped on a rug, fell, and hit his head on a nightstand. He bled to death and wasn't found for four days. Every detail of this haunts me. If I had called sooner, would we have spent time together? Might he have gotten busy getting to know me so that falling to his death on that lonely night wouldn't have happened? To stop myself from self-torture, I turn my mind back to the times that seemed more joyous, that live now only in photographs—the times when my godfather and other family members gathered comfortably in our living room.

Often, in studying those earlier times, I've thought, Where did everyone go? Why couldn't we be a family that maintained those connections, those bonds?

There was also, when I was a toddler, a train trip to Chicago to see relatives, which I have splintered memories of. It was a trip we only took that one time. A black-and-white photograph shows us disembarking from the train. Dad, you and Mom are holding me up and handing me down to my grandmother Edith. I'm assuming it was Loyal who was taking the picture. My expression is one of confusion and a slight tinge of fear, but everyone else is smiling. I don't remember much about that trip, but I can pull up images of tall buildings and a city that seemed gray and wintry. And, Dad, I have a thin memory of sitting on a balcony with you at night when you pointed out the North Star to me, telling me how it guided lost sailors home. Many decades later, when I took up pen and paper and decided my life would be lived as a writer, the theme of the North Star crept in often, both literally and metaphorically. I have always been able to find it in the night sky. What I never told you was that, for much of my life, I thought of you as my

North Star . . . until the skies got so crowded with reflected light, I couldn't find you anymore.

One of the constants of my childhood was seeing you on television every week as the host of *General Electric Theater*. Sometimes you would also act in one of the segments. There you were in your bathrobe opening the door late at night to a distraught and disheveled James Dean, who needed a doctor to treat his friend's bullet wound. I didn't always understand what was going on in these stories, but I was fascinated watching you. I had a vague understanding that because of General Electric, our new house that was being built only a few minutes from where we lived would be all electric, and part of your job was to do commercials for it. That last part was explained to me in an instructional way, and I pretended to understand.

I was about four when construction on that house began. We used to drive up and look at how things were coming along. Usually we'd take Lucky with us, and she and I would run up the hill in back. That house would come to be known as the General Electric House. It was on a narrow dead-end street, up a steep driveway on a hill that overlooked the city. I remember chilly days when I was bundled up in a jacket, and warm blue days when I was in shorts and a T-shirt, when dust puffed up in tiny clouds wherever I stepped.

There is one day that, when I watch it on film, fascinates me. There we are, Mom—mother and daughter dressed alike, in casual white pants and white short-sleeved shirts, holding hands as we walk around the construction site and then stand on the edge of the lot, looking at the city laid out below us. I don't know why I'm so fascinated by this, but I think it has to do with the fact that we were dressed in nearly identical clothes. I'd love to know how that came about. Did you just have a random idea that morning to dress me in clothes that mimicked yours? Or did the actress in you know that the home movies Dad would definitely be taking would look better if we were both in white, pinned against the backdrop of the sky and the faraway city? Whatever your thoughts were, it was sweet seeing us dressed alike, and a heart-breaking contrast to all that would emerge in the years that lay ahead of us, when your near-perfect fashion sense stood in contrast to a daughter who always seemed to be dressed incorrectly. Even when I tried to be fashionable, I would get it wrong. In 1983, at a dinner you and Dad gave for Queen Elizabeth, I splurged on a designer outfit only to have one journalist snipe: "There were 150 guests there. 149 of them were appropriately dressed."

Our last Christmas in the Amalfi house was when you almost burned the place down, Dad. It was actually just after Christmas, when trees and wreaths start drying out and need to be disposed of. For some reason, you thought that tossing the dried-up pine wreath into the fireplace was a good idea. Within seconds you realized it wasn't. Flames bulged out from the fireplace, the two of you ran into the kitchen, filled wastebaskets with water, and doused the flames. But there was a bigger problem—flames were shooting up from the chimney, sparks landing on the wood-shingle roof. The memory is so clear—Mom, me, and Lucky, who was barking furiously at all the commotion, huddled in the backyard as you, Dad, climbed up on the roof with a garden hose. I can still see you pinned against the sky, stars blinking around you, sparks bouncing at your feet as you aimed the hose, determined to save our home. It was cold that night, and Mom's arms were tight around me. For a moment I wondered if we would lose everything. But you doused all the sparks, hosed down the roof all around you, and when we went back inside there was the smell of wet ash, but no flames. It became a story you told in amusing tones, pointing out your

foolish mistake of tossing a wreath into the fireplace. What never became a part of the story was
how frightened we all were. But it was clear that
you were still the lifeguard, still the one to jump in
and save the day. I don't think you even called the
fire department.

All that heaven allows . . .

I DON'T RECALL the actual move into our new
home. I was five, and I know this was when I began
praying each night for a baby brother or sister.
The house was bigger than our old house; it made
my loneliness bigger too, as if it had grown ten-
drils. So, at night before bedtime when I dutifully
knelt beside my bed to talk to God, I asked Him
for a brother or sister, making clear I didn't care
which. I didn't want to burden Him with specific
demands, I just wanted someone to change the triangle of our family, to be my friend and compan-
ion. I trusted that somewhere in heaven, a brother
or sister was waiting to come down to earth and be
with me.

Fairly soon after we moved in, other people
arrived with cameras. We did several commercials
for General Electric with you, Mom, pretending to
know how to cook, which you in fact knew noth-

ing about. The camera crew would bring in piles of food, which was supposed to be what you had cooked, and I was told not to eat any of it because no one knew where it had been. Dad, you went on in detail about all the electrical features of the house and I was given a couple of lines to say, which I dutifully memorized. I had a little trouble pronouncing the word *electric*, but I did my best. There were other times when a photographer came with a couple of assistants and took still photos of us around the breakfast table, also piled with food I wasn't supposed to eat. I got used to sharing our lives with cameras. It seemed normal to me. But I think that's also when I began to understand that we had two lives—one we lived when the cameras were there, and the other we sometimes struggled through when we were alone. I can see, in those commercials, how hard I'm trying to be cute and endearing. I don't really know if that dichotomy existed with our home movies—did we alter ourselves when the Super 8 camera came out? I want to believe we didn't. I want to believe that those early innocent years were as full of love and joy as they appear to be. Your smile, Mom, in the home movies and early photographs, was different than your smile when we did commercials—less actressy. So, I'm going to settle on the decision that there was real, genuine affection during my baby and toddler years.

When you told me that my wishes had been answered, and you were going to have a baby, I not only thanked God in my nighttime prayers, I lay awake in the dark imagining a home with more laughter, more fun, because in our new house there didn't seem to be a lot of laughter.

My memories of your pregnancy are patchwork—some clear, some out of focus. What I do clearly recall is the last stage, when you were told by your doctor that you had to go on bed rest. You wore a pale pink bathrobe much of the time. You were soft and dreamy, and gentler than usual. Much later, I would wonder why you couldn't have stayed like that, your mouth in a perpetual half smile, your eyes kind, attentive.

When you brought Ron home from the hospital, I was shocked at how he looked. I'd never seen a newborn before, and I remember asking, "What's wrong with him?" He was tiny and wizened, his skin reddish. He definitely did not look like the babies on the bottles of Gerber baby food. I don't recall the answer to my question but I'm guessing it was something along the lines of, "That's how babies look when they're born." I watched him intently after that, seeing how he changed,

and imagining the life we would have together—
our bigger, more rounded-out family. But this was
when things began to change. This was when I
couldn't escape the pervasive feeling that I didn't
belong, I didn't fit in. There seemed to be only tension where once there had been warmth.

In trying to figure out the many versions of
you, Mom, I look for clues from your history—
the history that you tried to soften, sanitize. There
was the little girl—a baby, really—whose mother
abandoned her for six years, placing her with relatives, but that child wasn't someone you wanted to
acknowledge. I think she was always there, though,
waiting for you in quiet corners, with the roil of
emotions inside her that no one ever tended to.

When you were three years old, your mother—
divorced from your father and busy with her acting
career—decided you should go live with her sister
and brother-in-law, the Galbraiths, in Maryland.
Since your history was an ever-changing script, you
claimed in the redacted version that you completely
understood why your mother had to pursue her acting career and you harbored no resentment toward
her for her abandonment. What's come to fascinate
me in your renditions of events is how easily you set
logic aside. No three-year-old who is being abandoned by a parent has a comprehension of career

goals and why something this severe would become necessary. That young vulnerable child simply knows they are being cast aside by their parent. I find myself wondering, as you watched your mother driving away, if you thought, Maybe she'll turn around and come back, or maybe she'll be back tomorrow. Apparently Edith did visit occasionally, but never for very long, always leaving again to go back on the road and pursue the fame she craved. When you were nine, she visited and informed you that she had met a doctor whom she was going to marry, and you would be moving to Chicago with them. Another upheaval.

One cornerstone of the story you've told is that Loyal Davis, your new stepfather, wanted to adopt you early on, but Illinois law prohibited it until you were older. He did legally adopt you at fourteen, but I have never found anything saying that state law required him to wait until you were a teenager. The picture you painted, probably unwittingly, was of a young girl desperate for his love and attention. You said you went to the hospital and watched him perform surgery from the gallery, told him you wanted to be a nurse when you grew up.

Loyal Davis was an intimidating man. He had a stern mouth that curved downward and, even on the occasions when he laughed, the laughter seemed forced. His eyes never smiled. I was frankly terrified of him until the last year of his life when he somehow mysteriously mellowed a bit. It seems perfectly in character for him to have dangled adoption in front of you, withholding it for years, indulging himself in a cruel game of control and dominance, watching your desperate attempts to make him want you. I think now of the young girl you were, so starved for a commitment from him, and the tumult of emotions that you would spend a lifetime denying. It explains some of your anger, and since anger needs a focus, I became that focus.

I look even further back in your history to find the blueprint for who you became as a mother. I think about the infant who was carried around from city to city by a mother whose acting career was her main priority. Being a stage actress in the twenties was not an easy life, especially if you were a stock player, as Edith (then Edith Luckett) was. There was train travel, backstage dressing rooms that were far from glamorous, run-down hotel rooms. I don't recall who told me this—maybe it was you, Mom—but somewhere I heard that as a baby you were often put to sleep in a dresser drawer lined with blankets backstage in whatever theater your mother was working in.

There is an intimacy to babyhood, or there should

be. Bodily functions have to be tended to, babies cry to be held, long to be nurtured. Those babies grow into people who have no actual memory of their infancy but who are, nonetheless, molded by it. I don't know if, once you got to the Galbraiths, you were given affection. Were you tended to in all the ways that a three-year-old needs to be? Who potty-trained you? Who came into your room in the dead of night when you woke up crying from a bad dream? Or sat with you when you were sick? Did anyone? Because somehow, over time, those aspects of motherhood became a burden to you, and I think now that the needs I had as a child unearthed the needs that were never met in your own childhood.

It's somewhat startling when we realize that our parents had lives before they became our parents—often complicated lives, with pain and loneliness and unresolved trauma. We start to understand, once we're older, that the only way to inch past the turbulence that was injected into our own lives is to figure out the art of forgiveness. That isn't an easy task, it isn't as if there is a manual for it. It's like learning a dance with no accompanying music; we stumble, get confused, search for a rhythm that will anchor us.

In *Prince of Tides*, Pat Conroy writes, "If your parents disapprove of you and are cunning with their disapproval, there will never come a new dawn when you can become convinced of your own value. There is no fixing a damaged childhood. The best you can hope for is to make the sucker float."

It was after we moved into our new house on the hill that my nosebleeds started. They happened when the weather turned dry; it was explained to me that I had a blood vessel in my nose that would dry out and break, then start to bleed. But understanding the cause did nothing to ease my terror. The nosebleeds would happen at night. I'd wake up on a wet pillow, turn on the lamp, and see that I'd been lying in a pool of blood. The first couple of times I screamed, and you both came running in, took me to the bathroom, had me tilt my head back and squeeze my nose shut with a washcloth until the bleeding stopped. When it became a more common occurrence, you'd come into my bedroom alone, Mom, and we would go through the same ritual. By that time, I had started to feel self-conscious, as if I were becoming a burden, an inconvenience. I had overheard you one afternoon talking with a friend of yours about my tendency to have nosebleeds. Your friend said that I must "really have it in for you" to keep putting you through this, and you agreed. I remember wishing I were old enough to just walk out of the house and leave; that way I wouldn't be such a weight on your life.

One night, you and Dad were out to dinner and a babysitter was there when it happened. She was trying to help me, and I told her I wanted to die and go live with the angels. She was upset by what I'd said, and when the two of you got home, she told you about it. You laughed and told her that I was just being dramatic. "That's just what my daughter does," you said, your words balanced on trills of laughter. What I want you to know is, when I told the babysitter that I wanted to die, I meant it. I have a clear memory of feeling like I was becoming so inconvenient, I wanted to go to the faraway land of heaven that Dad always described as being green and peaceful, with calm waters and God hovering protectively over everyone. In my child's imagination no one had nosebleeds there and everyone was happy and nice to one another.

Sometimes going through the life we've lived is like scooping up handfuls of broken glass, trying to see different reflections in the various pieces.

Some of the reflections I have come to see, Mom, are those of your own childhood, or at least the parts of it that I know. Your mother leaving you with her sister and brother-in-law says in fairly certain terms that you were becoming a burden. Your cousin, whom you grew up with in those years, visited us sometimes. Charlotte Galbraith Ramage would come to California occasionally with her husband; I vaguely knew she was your cousin, but I never heard the two of you share memories. It was as if you had locked away those vulnerable years of your life and tossed away the key. But life doesn't work like that. Our experiences remain alive in us, even if we try to ignore them or rewrite them.

Both you and Dad flinched from memories that caused pain in your past. It's a skill set that each of you mastered, probably before you even met. You were well suited to each other in many ways, and reconfiguring the past was one of those ways.

Our new home had a swimming pool, and we spent so much time in and around the pool, I think my fingers were permanently crinkled from the chlorine water. Ron had the required swimming lessons, I learned to dive off the board, and Lady, our rescue shepherd, would occasionally dive into the water. We laughed and splashed our way through summers. Ron was a happy child, always delighted by everything. Dad, you even started calling him "Happy Jack." In our home movies, he was a tiny bundle of energy and always smiling.

But there was a dark tide moving in beneath us, and it belonged mainly to you and me, Mom. In all the home movies of us swimming and playing in the pool, there is one brief moment that reveals where we had come to and where we were headed. Mom, you are holding a raft with Ron on it, the two of you are laughing. I swim over to join in, but you push me away. The movies are without sound, so I have no idea what was said, but the visual image is emblematic of the relationship we would carry into the future.

It wasn't long before I turned not-smiling into an art form. There is film from later—I must have been about eleven—where I am standing in the driveway with you and Ron. We are obviously headed somewhere, and I'm guessing it was to the annual May Day festivities at our school because both Ron and I are dressed in white. He looks fairly neutral, not as bubbly as he was when he was younger, but my face is set in a determined scowl. You are standing between us, talking to Dad, who is behind the camera, and you're visibly annoyed. It's easy to read your lips. "She won't smile," you're saying. "She just won't smile." Scowling became my signature expression as time went on; I advertised my unhappiness both at home and in school.

Anger was the shield I held up to try to protect myself in battle, since the battles between you and me were becoming so inescapable. It was an inadequate shield—you would always be the victor—but it was all I had. Your anger toward me was an ever-present thing; even when it was hidden from view, I knew it was there. I waited for it to emerge, and it was formidable. You didn't let it out when Dad was around, at least not that I ever saw. I never witnessed or overheard a fight between the two of you, and it's possible that he didn't even believe you had a temper, since he had a talent for not seeing what he didn't want to see. It was a destructive dance that ensnared you and me, and it happened mostly when Dad went out of town for his General Electric business trips. I came to realize that it didn't matter what I did or didn't do, you were going to lash out at me. With six years difference between me and Ron, he was in his own baby and then toddler world, so it often felt like it was just the two of us in that house, on a collision course that nothing could alter. I visualized your anger as embers glowing with heat that would explode into flames with the slightest wind. Unfortunately, I seemed to be that wind.

Many times, your temper would flare in the car when it was just the two of us. I remember trying to calculate how I could avoid this. I would stay quiet, stare out the passenger-side window, but my silence was regarded as hostility, and you would get angry at that. One incident I recall is actually rather funny now. We were coming home and were very near our street. You were yelling at me and driving over the speed limit when a police car came up behind us and we heard the siren. You pulled over, composed yourself, and switched on your infectious charm as the policeman came to the window. Calmly, sweetly, you explained to him that your daughter was just being impossible, had tried your patience and made you stomp down on the accelerator without realizing it. The officer nodded understandingly, looked harshly at me, and told me to behave myself and stop upsetting my mother. Predictably, he didn't give you a ticket.

Ironically, there was a portrait of the two of us hanging in your bedroom, right over the fireplace. I think I'm about three or four. You're leaning in to me, your head tilted down and your mouth curved in a Mona Lisa–like smile. Your eyes look loving and calm—the same eyes I see in our early home movies. I look like I'm staring off into nothing. I remember slivers of that day when we sat for the artist. There was a winding metal staircase that took us to a shadowy room where a man told us to sit in uncomfortable chairs. I have a vague memory of him telling me to smile, which I apparently didn't. That painting greeted me whenever I walked into your and Dad's room, a memory in portraiture of how we once were with each other.

Someone once said to me that they thought the reason you didn't like me was because I was the flaw in your romantic illusion with Dad, and there might be some truth to that. The story you have told about you and Dad has the two of you being instantly smitten, falling head over heels in love and never looking back. You even used phrases like "my world began when I met Ronnie." But the reality was a bit different. From everything I've heard, Dad wasn't entirely exclusive to you, and as a newly divorced man he was not exactly anxious to get married again. In fact, he had made an agreement with Jane Wyman that he wouldn't remarry before she did. You were a good girlfriend—going out to the ranch with him to do tedious tasks like painting fences and sitting in the jeep while he built jumps. You got on horses even though riding was never your thing. Often Michael and Maureen would go out with you; Michael remembers sitting in your lap in the station wagon. (There weren't seat belts in the fifties.)

But there was no marriage proposal . . . until you told Dad you were pregnant. You told him over dinner at Chasen's Restaurant and, according to Michael, Dad excused himself, used the restaurant phone to call Jane and tell her, mostly because he didn't think he could honor the agreement he'd made with her. I wonder if you ever knew about that call. So many things about this still astound me. Knowing how resolutely you set your sights on what you wanted, I tend to doubt that getting pregnant was a result of carelessness. But your calculations were fraught with risk. Dad could have said the baby wasn't his. There was no DNA testing then, so he could have claimed the baby was someone else's. And in the fifties, a single woman being pregnant invited scandal, resulted in her being ostracized. When Ingrid Bergman got pregnant by Roberto Rossellini while both were married to other people, a U.S. senator took to the floor of the Senate in 1950 and called her "a powerful influence for evil." She essentially became a pariah in Hollywood, at least for a while. In a rare moment of bravery, I asked you once, when I was in my forties, what you would have done if Dad had refused to marry you when you told him you were pregnant. Without missing a beat, you said, "I knew he wouldn't do that." Which says so much about you. That confidence was the heartbeat of your power, and I don't know where you got it. The toddler who was shuffled off to relatives, the little girl who lived with a family not her own, who never spoke about those childhood years except to say that she was overweight and clumsy, somehow manufactured a confidence in her own machinations that refused to entertain the notion of failure. I never stood a chance with you.

I've often wondered if you ever accepted that Dad once loved Jane Wyman. While it's true that the marriage failed after nine years, they married because they fell in love. I wonder if you ever watched any of her films, if you gave her credit for being the brilliant actress that she was. I'm fairly certain that if you did watch her films, you didn't tell Dad about it. Your technique for dealing with his past was to pretend he didn't have one; that's why Michael and Maureen were so inconvenient. Jane Wyman won an Academy Award for the film *Johnny Belinda*, in which she played a deaf-mute. You said often that you gave up your career when you got married, but you were competitive in your acting years, and I suspect Jane's Oscar didn't sit well with you.

She also did a film with Rock Hudson called *All That Heaven Allows* in which she plays a wealthy widow who falls in love with the gardener, played by Rock Hudson. She's looked down upon by the town for the relationship, and so she leaves him. But love prevails and she finds her way back to him, committing to their relationship at the end after he suffers an accidental fall and almost dies. I find the title so evocative, especially if I apply it to our family. Heaven allowed you to meet the man you called your "soulmate" and stay locked in a love that didn't need anyone but the two of you. It allowed you to stand with him as he rose into the rarefied air of those who will forever be immortalized in history. The most insightful thing I ever heard you say was one day when Dad was adrift in the mysterious seas Alzheimer's had carried him into, and you were reflecting on what you had lost. You then said, "I don't think I appreciated what I had when I had it. At least not enough." I didn't respond to you; I let your words linger between us. I said nothing because I believed you were right.

It was a moment of softness—of vulnerability and self-awareness—that both surprised and impressed me. You were so often intimidating, not just to me but to so many others. I've watched people quake in your presence. If I imagine you in other careers, I think you'd have made a good CIA agent—you could have rooted out the enemy and figured out their vulnerabilities in seconds. Or the head of a small country, ruling it like Eva Perón, mixing an iron fist with fluttering eyelashes.

Looking back from where I am now, I see that

my attempt to defend myself with anger was a fool's errand. But it was the only thing that helped me through the arctic winters of your disapproval. As my life went on, though, anger became my downfall. It ruined romantic relationships, turned me down the wrong paths, blinded me. I had birthed it so long ago I didn't know how to rid myself of it. Finally, something dawned on me. I decided to try thanking that anger, showing it gratitude for helping me get through the years when you would have hobbled me so severely I wouldn't have recovered. It had been a lifeline and I'd hung on to it like anyone afraid of drowning would. But, having recognized that, having thanked it for saving me, I then had to say: I don't need you anymore. It's not who I want to be now.

This epiphany happened while you were still here; you were in failing health and my weekend visits to you often felt like gambling with a losing hand. Sometimes you were friendly and warm, happy to see me, other times not. I never stopped being afraid of you, but I stopped reaching for that lifeline of anger because I'd finally decided that your disapproval was no longer going to pull me down into quicksand. I was stronger than that. On one of those visits, when you were mostly bedridden, you were being particularly aggressive with me. You had scheduled another visitor that day—a man you had known since he was a boy, and whom I had grown up around. I knew once he got there that you would soften and be nicer. When the Secret Service called and said he'd arrived, I hurriedly went outside to get a few moments alone with him. I told him it had been a rough afternoon so far, and he asked me why I visited so often when you made the visits difficult. I told him that I believed you and I had gone through lifetimes together, and that I wanted this to be the last one. I wanted resolution, an end to whatever ravages had scarred the landscape of our past. I wanted off the karmic wheel we were on, and the only way I knew to accomplish that was to show up. He still reminds me of that conversation.

Going back . . .

IT WAS AFTER YOU DIED, Dad, when I was trying to figure out who Mom and I were going to be to each other without you there to draw us together, that I began going to our old neighborhood in Pacific Palisades. I've become a familiar figure there now, walking up hills that used to be dirt trails but are now paved and lined with houses.

I see again the young girl whose father removed

the training wheels from her bicycle and encouraged her to ride to the end of the cul-de-sac. It was a gray, wintry day, and you were standing beside James Arness, of *Gunsmoke* fame, who had just moved onto the street. As I carefully turned around and started pedaling back toward you, I was struck by how handsome and invincible the two of you seemed. Two tall, confident men standing in the damp air watching their kids. I used to often say, "My Daddy can do anything." You and Mom thought it was cute and always smiled. But to me, it was an irrefutable truth.

I linger sometimes at the intersection of four streets where there is a wide area in the middle. That was the location of one of my more indelible dreams in which I had heard that God would be passing by at that exact spot, right where the four streets intersected. I stood there waiting for Him, but He never came. I never told you about that dream, Dad, because it cut so deep. It was how I often felt growing up—that I was waiting for God, but He had forgotten about me. Deciphering the dream has gotten easier for me over the years—I didn't think you and Mom liked me very much, and if that was the case, why would God care about me? I longed to have the experience you spoke about, Dad, when you were a young actor doing a film in England. You said you woke up suddenly one night, jolted by something unseen, unknown. You sat up in bed and suddenly you felt ghostly hands on your shoulders that gave you the most profound sense of security and safety. You believed they were God's hands. I used to ask you why you didn't turn around and look, and you would always say you didn't need to, you knew who was there. I longed to have such an experience, but I had no faith that I ever would.

My dream about waiting in the intersection of streets also marked the point at which I stopped talking to you about God. Throughout my childhood, God, angels, and the blue waters of heaven formed the threads of many of our conversations. But as I started to feel you drift away, as I was haunted by the fear that God had abandoned me, I no longer talked to you about my dreams or my questions about the world beyond this one. Apparently that registered with you, because decades later, when you were slipping away into Alzheimer's, I said something to you about prayer and you looked shocked. "Well, I'm happy to hear you say that," you said. "I just assumed you didn't believe in God anymore."

Sometimes what we fail to say has as much impact as what we do say.

-<-<--->->

As Ron delighted you both with his amiable nature, the intractable war between you and me, Mom, kept brewing, often to a boil. The discord between us was matched only by your bitterness toward Michael. I felt sorry for him, but I did not dare speak up and defend him—I had too much tension of my own to deal with. I came to understand, even at a fairly young age, that the problem you had with him was that he was a reminder of what you didn't want to acknowledge—there had been another Mrs. Reagan before you. Michael had come to live with us, yet he didn't have an actual room. While it was true that we didn't have a spare bedroom, since we had live-in help and the room off the kitchen was hers, it would have been possible to put a bed in Ron's room and have them share space, but if that was ever considered, it wasn't done. So, Michael slept on the living room couch and used the powder room, as if he were a guest. Mom, you announced that we would now be eating fish on Fridays because he was Catholic and it was a requirement of the Catholic Church. You said it as if this concession were proof that he was now part of our family. But he wasn't really included; that was made very clear. In one of our home movies, he's playing with Ron in the backyard as if we are a happy, united clan. But the thing about the camera is, it captures a moment in time and, as truthful as that moment might be, there are other moments, not recorded, that reveal different truths. We were never comfortable around each other. With or without Michael, there was never a feeling of ease between us, a sense of belonging. It was as if we were strangers forced to live in a house together with no clue how to make it feel like a home.

Yet when we were by the water, somehow the four of us seemed to mend. Each summer, we drove to San Diego to stay at the Hotel del Coronado— its elegance and formal decor harkening back to the Edwardian Age. Before Ron was born, the three of us would make the long car drive—longer then because the freeway hadn't yet been built—and we would stay one night in La Jolla to break up the journey. In Coronado, we'd meet up with a family whom we never saw any other time of the year. They were names on Christmas cards whom we saw in person only during that one week in summer. I still don't know what your history was with them. By the time Ron could go with us, it was a faster trip on the newly constructed freeway and our days would be spent swimming in the ocean, walking along the shore, and lounging on the sand. Michael, though, never went with us on these trips, and I asked him decades later where he went instead. So many times he just vanished, and I knew I wasn't supposed to ask where he was. He told me he was sent away to camp for much of the summer.

Our other summer ritual was to rent a house on Trancas Beach, north of Malibu, for a couple of weeks. Dad, that's where you taught me to bodysurf, to head straight out toward waves that, frankly, looked terrifying. But I trusted that the instructions you were giving me would allow me to catch the wave and ride it into shore. With the sound of the sea loud around us, you would shout out, "Turn now! Swim!" And I would obediently turn my back to the swelling wall of water behind me, swim furiously until I felt the wave lift me and slide me down its front, where it would push me— my arms pressed tight at my sides, my body straight as an arrow—safely to the beach. I knew you were riding the same wave, and even though I couldn't see you through the water, I felt safe knowing we inhabited the same wedge of ocean right then. I didn't always get it right. I remember once, when a particularly large wave crashed on top of me and sent me swirling down beneath the surface, I came up gasping for breath and you were there, treading water, your eyes full of worry and pieces of sunlight. "Where'd you go?" you asked. I keep that moment now in my heart because I saw how concerned you were, and I cherished that. The man, the lifeguard, who often seemed obscured by mist and distance was there in the churning white foam scanning the seawater looking anxiously for his daughter to burst through the surface.

It's how it always was, and still is—grabbing on to moments, slivers of time, keeping them polished and safe in my memory. Sometimes the father who was perpetually out of reach would be right there, helping me off the ground after my horse threw me or waiting in the sea for me to fight to the surface. Those moments were few, but they are part of our story.

Mom, those weeks in Trancas thawed the ever-present cold war that divided us. As I said, we were always better when we were by water. It's as if we were washed clean, for a while at least. You and I would take walks on the beach sometimes. I don't remember now what we talked about, or if we talked at all. I just remember a feeling of seren-ity. Here is something that will surprise you: From the time I was a little girl, I daydreamed about us being friends, about us spending time together as I saw my school friends do with their mothers—easy, uncomplicated time. At the beach, with the tides changing and sea spray washing over us, I could pretend that was who we were. But I always knew I was pretending. We would return to our battlefield, because that was where we were anchored—on hard dry ground, far from the forgiveness of the sea.

When we were at the beach, the dinner table conversations revolved around the surf, the great waves we rode. Sometimes we'd talk about a school of dolphins that had glided by, mesmerizing us with their journey. It was so different from our life at home, where politics had started to dominate everything. Politics was a tangible presence, as if it had a seat at our table and competed with me for your attention, Dad. I think that became stunningly real around 1960, when Kennedy and Nixon were locked in a race for president. You talked about Nixon often, about how the country needed him and how he would be a historically important president. I remember you and Mom watching the debate on television between Nixon and Kennedy and I didn't understand how a man who talked funny and was so stiff could be appealing to you; I did understand when election night came that Kennedy would be our new president.

Not too long after the election, I was told one

morning as I boarded the school bus that I was not to go into my room that afternoon when I came home. Mr. Nixon is coming over for dinner, you both explained, and he'll be coming straight from the airport, so he will need to clean up and change clothes, and he'll be using your room. That afternoon, when I got home, I heard the two of you and Nixon talking in the den, so I went straight to my room to see what he had done in there. His clothes were laid out on the twin bed and when I inspected them, I didn't see any underwear. I raced into the kitchen, where Cora, our housekeeper, was preparing dinner. I loved Cora—she hugged me a lot and taught me how to bake cookies. On rainy days, she made me tomato soup and grilled cheese sandwiches. I felt like I could ask her anything. One day I asked her why the palms of her hands were pink when the rest of her skin was black. She pulled me against her, ruffled my hair, and said, "Because God has a lot of colors to use, and he likes to use different ones."

"Cora," I whispered fiercely. "Mr. Nixon is wearing dirty underwear."

I can still picture her stifling a laugh. But she composed herself, bent down, and put her hands on my shoulders. "Child, don't you go saying that to anyone. You hear me? Not to anyone. Now, you go in there and say hello, and say something nice to Mr. Nixon."

I would do anything Cora told me. She was the one person in the house whom I obeyed without question. So, I went into the den—into ice clinking in glasses and the music of adult voices. I shook Nixon's hand and said, "I'm sorry you lost the election."

"Well," he said, "thank you. But if I hadn't lost, I wouldn't be here tonight."

I wasn't sure what that meant. Were presidents not allowed to go into people's homes? In any event, I obeyed Cora, I never breathed a word about Mr. Nixon's underwear to anyone, especially not to the two of you. I ate in the kitchen that night and I could hear through the door the conversation about politics—that intruder who had come to stay. I longed for summer, for watching dolphins in the ocean, for an escape from the incessant talk about big government and those pesky Communists.

One year I overheard the two of you talking in your bedroom, questioning whether you could afford to take us to the beach that summer. What I learned by eavesdropping was that you, Dad, had just been fired from *General Electric*. It was 1962, I was ten years old, I had grown up watching you on television every Sunday night on *General Electric*

Theater. You were the host, and sometimes you were one of the star actors. Now you were being fired? It was years later before I understood why, and that required some homework on my part.

I had become accustomed to you being away on short promotional trips for GE—usually about four or five days. I assumed you were doing the same thing we did in the commercials, talking effusively about the all-electric world of GE, touting its impressive appliances. But as it turns out, you were not talking about washing machines and ovens. You were actually honing the political speech that would, years later, be called "A Time for Choosing" and would propel you into national politics, changing our lives forever. Originally, though, the speech was called "Business, Ballots, and Bureaus." It wasn't exactly what the bigwigs at GE were sending you out on the road for. From what I understand, you gave the speech to a gathering of GE executives and that led to you being fired. Fortunately, we did still go to the ocean for our summer vacation, and neither of you ever mentioned the firing. I was only told about it later when you were going out to the ranch almost every day.

Something else happened in 1962. Nelle died. It was just past the middle of summer, late July, and my memory is that the two of you told me together, but I only recall looking at you, Dad. I knew how much you loved your mother, how you revered her, and she was the one family member I longed to know better. But once she was put into a facility, there was just that one strange visit—the dingy green walls and strange-smelling air, nurses padding in and out. I have a memory of touching her hand—it was cold, thin. Her eyes seemed far away. It was the last time I saw her before learning that she had died.

I never heard about a service for her. Over the years I have tried to research whether or not there was one. Certainly Ron and I didn't go to one, which is also strange. I was ten and he was four; we were old enough to attend a funeral for our grandmother. It was hard for me to believe, Dad, that you would have buried her without any kind of ceremony. Finally, very recently a writer friend who is better at research than I am found the mention of a service in the *Los Angeles Times* from July 1962. "On Friday July 26th," it read, "at 2 PM there will be a service for Nelle Reagan at the Hollywood Beverly Christian Church." I will never know now who attended, and why Ron and I weren't included. The only other information I have is that Nelle is buried next to Jack at a cemetery in Los Angeles. I wish Nelle were not in that crowded purgatory of unanswered questions that our family has created, but there she is. I will never understand the reasoning. Weren't you exhausted from all the things you hid and didn't speak about?

Secrets...

OUR OTHER STANDARD VACATION—at Easter, when we would travel to Arizona to stay with your parents, Mom—was not one I eagerly anticipated. Edith and Loyal both frightened me, but for different reasons. It's probably not surprising to you that Loyal Davis was intimidating—he was known to have that effect on almost everyone. The stern, precise neurosurgeon with the thin unsmiling mouth and steely eyes. A memory that pops up is of him in the laundry room in Phoenix wrapping packages to mail. Every corner had to be perfect, every piece of string tied to perfection, and the tape was placed in an unwavering line. It's how he went through life, and it's how he treated other people. You acted as if you weren't scared of him, but I knew you were. It was there in the way you obediently brought him his coffee, with just the right dollop of cream in it. And the way you laughed even when he was mocking you.

My fear of Edith is something I have never told

anyone about. It trailed me through the years and was the reason I committed what you deemed an unforgivable sin—not attending her funeral service. Even though I ultimately apologized, several people have told me that you would mention often how I had not come to your mother's funeral and how bitter you were about it. Clearly, it was something for which you never forgave me. So, I want you to know the real reason why I didn't come, the secret I've held on to all this time. Before I get to that, though, I want to go to the easier memories of Phoenix, the ones that look more like postcards.

We traveled by train because you were afraid to fly, Dad—a fear you willed yourself to muscle past many years later when you were running for governor. But in my childhood years, that fear meant we boarded the Super Chief in the evening, slept on the train in small cabins, one for me and Ron, one for you and Mom. The *Super Chief* was as elegant as a train can get—men dressed as butlers taking passengers to their cabins, crisp white tablecloths, crystal glasses and shiny silverware in the dining car. I slept in the upper part of the bunk bed. Ron would drift off to sleep quickly, I could hear his breathing, and I would lie awake. I'd open the little sliding door over the window and rest on my side watching the land whir by, the dark, seemingly endless miles dotted sometimes with lights from houses scattered in what seemed like perpetual wilderness. I would doze and then wake up again, always in time to see the screen of a drive-in movie as we passed it. I remember thinking how vast the country seemed, and how full of lives it was—lives I would never know anything about. We would have breakfast the next morning in the gleaming dining car and I don't know how I always ended up with pancakes because I could never finish them. There was an enormous helping of them on my plate and just seeing them was so overwhelming my stomach closed up. The train always made a stop in Yuma. We would get off and find a group of Native Americans sitting beside the train tracks selling beaded trinkets and blankets. Dad, you always bought something from one of the women and gave it to me—a beaded coin purse or a bracelet. I felt bad for the people sitting in the dust, the sun beating down on them, trying to earn a little money. The images stayed with me, haunted me a bit as we disembarked in Phoenix and headed for my grandparents' house on the golf course.

The memories are still lucid—how their backyard was literally the golf course, how the sprinklers in the evening hissed across the grass. Quail called out early in the morning and rabbits scampered under the hedges. We went horseback riding at a nearby stable, where an aged cowboy had false teeth that were loose and moved every time he spoke. I know you weren't happy riding there, Dad—flat miles of dry desert, a western saddle instead of the English saddle you preferred, no trees to shade us or lakes to bring calm to the terrain. But it was only a faint look in your eyes that gave it away. You were always so gracious.

There is a story that's evolved in the public domain in which Loyal Davis was the political muse who turned your views more to the right. I've even heard it said that he was responsible for you leaving the Democratic Party and becoming a Republican. I've never believed that, and I have no memories of him launching into any kind of political dialogue. I do recall the conversations you instigated—the same ones you had started to introduce around our dining room table at home. Conversations about Communists, and the danger they posed to all of America, to our way of life and our freedom. This always confused me. I didn't know any Communists; no one ever said where they lived or how they could be identified, and the most baffling thing to me was that I had learned in history class about America welcoming all points of view. Didn't that mean the Communists got to be here too? I didn't dare ask about this, since the whole subject seemed to be so fraught, the implication being that the country itself was in grave danger. But my memories of my grandfather are that he listened, agreed with you, perhaps injected some observations of his own, but I don't think he ever proselytized.

Mom, there was never a chance that I could have shared with you why I was frightened of your mother. First, you wouldn't have believed me, and second, I would have gotten in trouble for what you would have deemed a lie. But now, with the finality of death between us, I can describe what happened.

The fear first took hold of me when I was about eight or nine. I needed to ask Edith something and I went down the hall into their bedroom. The door was ajar, as was the door to the bathroom, and I heard running water. I peeked in and saw her bent over the sink as if she were brushing her teeth. I spoke her name and she turned to me, opening her mouth wide so that I would see she had no teeth. I had no idea before this that she had false teeth, and the sight of her cavernous toothless mouth scared the hell out of me. I don't remember if I screamed, but I did start running away down the hall, and she chased me, witch-like, laughing. I raced outside onto the golf course and ran as fast as I could to my friend's place two houses away. They had a swimming pool; I think I needed to be by water, since water was the balm that so often healed the wounds in our family. But it didn't heal this one. Fear had set up residency inside me. Edith started doing things at the dinner table that I would never have gotten away with—opening her mouth with food in it, always in my direction. Inexplicably, everyone else laughed. I was the only one at the table who didn't find it funny.

Unlike my friends, I developed early. I was the first girl in my grade school class to get a bra. (They were called training bras then.) I was eleven. That's when my fear of your mother intensified and clamped down on me like a vise. Because when we went to Phoenix, or when she and Loyal came to visit us at Christmas, she would grab my still-developing breasts and make crude comments about how big I was getting. She then started grabbing me between my legs, asking if I had started my period yet. It was always when no one else was around, so I knew I could never say anything about it and be believed. I tried to avoid being alone with her, but I wasn't always successful. For decades, I never told anyone about it—not a friend or a therapist, not a religious counselor, not my husband. *No one.* It was embarrassing, shameful, and the idea that I wouldn't be believed followed me through the years.

As I write this, another question comes to mind. Did Edith exhibit the same behavior with you? She came back for you when you were nine, but your years of maturing into a woman were in front of you and you went through them under her roof. It seems unlikely that I was the only person she handled so invasively.

When Edith died in 1987, and her funeral was planned in Phoenix, I had no desire to pretend that I was mourning, nor did I think I even had the ability to act the part of a grieving granddaughter. So, I lied. I told everyone that I had a business commitment out of the country and would be unable to attend. Years later, my apology to you, Mom, was simply that—no explanation attached to it. This is what I want to say now: I should have gone. If I were the person then that I am now, I would have gone to the funeral of the woman who haunted me, who touched me where she shouldn't have, because you don't get past life's scars by running away. You get past them by walking right up to them, being the bigger person, and staring them down. I was not that person then. The truth is that I did the best I was capable of at the time.

Maya Angelou said, "Do the best you can until

you know better. Then, when you know better, do better." It's a good mantra for how to live life.

It was on one of those Easter vacations, in 1964, that I heard for myself the speech that would catapult you, Dad, into politics. By then the speech had been re-titled "A Time for Choosing." You were campaigning for Barry Goldwater and you gave the speech in a school auditorium. I can still picture it—the fluorescent lighting, the hard chairs, and people around me wearing little straw hats with Goldwater banners on them. I remember kids too, who appeared to have Clearasil on their faces. But my deepest memory is listening to you. I knew instinctually that this was going to change our lives forever. Your grip on the audience was unmistakable, you had them mesmerized. I was twelve years old, and I was sitting in an auditorium on a fold-up metal chair watching my father leave me. Politics, my enemy, was taking you away.

<del>◄-►</del>

I DIDN'T KNOW IT during those Easter vacations, but Arizona was about to become my home for the entirety of high school. Since I had become a discipline problem in school, frequently being insubordinate and getting in trouble, it was decided I would go to a co-ed boarding school in a remote part of Arizona—seventy miles north of Phoenix, near Flagstaff, but really it wasn't near anything. It was a functioning cattle ranch and twice a year we were required to participate in rounding up the cows. High school was when I stopped eating beef. One advantage to the school was that the teachers were given free rein to teach how and what they wanted, so the education I got there was way beyond what is usually found in high school. I also got to take my horse; I was one of about three students who rode English on this western cattle ranch, and I spent more time with Quicksilver than I did with other people.

The disadvantages, one could say, were that 180 kids, stuck out in the desert, were bound to get in all sorts of trouble. Someone figured out how to grow pot, cigarettes were passed to kids who were way too young to be smoking, and the hay barn became the chosen spot to lose one's virginity. I spent my first couple of years getting in rather minor trouble, having decided it seemed cool to sneak a cigarette with other kids even though smoking made me feel sick. When we all got caught (useful tip: spraying deodorant in a bathroom after you've smoked doesn't remove the evidence) we were punished with work hours and our parents were notified. Those were the occasions when I got lengthy letters from you, Dad, telling me about the health risks of smoking and the importance of adhering to the rules. I've wondered since if maybe I consciously got in trouble so I could get your attention.

By then your attention was focused on much bigger, more important things. You were running for governor when I went away to school, and I wasn't there long before election night came around and you became the next governor of California. I didn't behave very well that night when you and Mom called me.

The way the phone system worked at my boarding school was, if someone called a student, their name would be announced over the loudspeaker that boomed through the barnyard and reached the rustic dorm rooms. Then that student would go to an outside phone booth by the office buildings and take the call. It was cold that November night; our school was far enough north that the seasons were well defined. Autumn brought cold, sharp winds and turned the leaves yellow on the few trees that were there. Winter brought snow, sometimes several feet of it; one winter we were snowed in and the power went out. I remember on this night walking across the barnyard alone, knowing who would be on the phone and what I would hear. Your voice, Dad, was happy, elated.

"We won! I wanted you to know," you said. I bristled at the word *we*. I was already crying before I picked up the phone, but I started crying harder. I said something like, "But I didn't want this for my life." Clearly a rather immature response—and selfish—but I had just turned fifteen and I was looking ahead at a life that seemed predestined and controlled by forces I didn't trust and knew little about. So, I apologize for my selfishness in that moment, but at fifteen I don't think I could have done any better. At some point that night I had a premonition that would follow me for years as your political career expanded almost exponentially. I thought of Abraham Lincoln getting assassinated in Ford Theatre and I had the eerie but unmistakable feeling that you too were going to get shot. Fourteen years later, when John Hinckley almost killed you, I was that young girl again, standing in a blue-white pool of light in a phone booth with fear rising in me and a feeling of dread about what fate had in store for all of us.

The end of innocence . . .

THE MOST LIFE-CHANGING DRAMA of my years away came in my junior year. He was tall and athletic, with blond hair and sharp blue eyes that seemed to see everything. He was my English teacher and my tennis coach. His flirtations with me were erudite and irresistible. He nurtured my writing, probably helped mold me as a writer, and he would claim control over my life for the next three years. He would also end up, Mom, being the catalyst for one of the only bonding interludes we ever had.

I still have a copy of the first poem I wrote about him—the one I handed him one night in study hall when he was the teacher assigned there. I was writing only poetry then and he helped me believe that I could be successful, published, read by many. The poem I handed him began: "Again, caught by blue eyes and a soft touch, caution is too narrow a commitment." I can still picture him reading it and looking at me across the room, the blue of his eyes looking like the future I thought would be mine. It sounds so foolish now, a seventeen-year-old girl and a man in his thirties, married, with two children. But at seventeen, dreams ripen easily. To make matters even more complicated, he had me babysit his kids sometimes and I genuinely cared about his wife and children. I convinced myself that this triangle of emotions—for him, but also for his wife, and their kids—was something that could make sense, that did make sense. I tried to fit it into the mold of some of the literary works we studied in his class. I think at one point I decided it was Shakespearean, this cauldron of feelings that I believed could find some sort of harmony.

When his wife was away, when the kids were asleep, we fooled around, but never consummated the relationship. That latter part is all I told you, Mom, when years later we talked about it. What I didn't tell you is that, when I turned eighteen, I thought, Maybe we can now really become lovers. After all, I'm no longer a minor, I'm no longer jailbait. But then I thought, I'm a virgin—he might not want to be the one to take my virginity. So, on one of our Easter Vacations in Phoenix, I went on a date with a boy I'd been playing tennis with at the Biltmore Hotel and I lost my virginity in his tiny one-room apartment with brick walls and a single sagging bed. He ran out to the gas station to get a condom before we took the final step of "going all the way." It was unfair to this boy, because I didn't really care about him, I just wanted to get it over with so that I would be able to be with the man I loved so desperately. That night, I had told you and Dad that my date and I were going to a movie—*Lawrence of Arabia*—and I did some homework on the film so I could pretend the next day that I'd actually seen it.

When spring break ended and I returned to my boarding school, I told the man who had enveloped my world that I was no longer a virgin, and now that I was eighteen, I hoped we could consummate our relationship. It still didn't happen. He was an expert at taking me to the edge and then leaving me there.

One night he took me to a different kind of edge, a more dangerous one. He had a motorbike and in the late hours we met up at a remote spot past the barnyard. I hopped on back and we rode out into the desert. It was a moonless night, the darkness vast and unforgiving. He took us up to the unpaved airstrip that the school kept in case anyone ever needed to be airlifted out by helicopter. The strip cut through the night, heading deeper into the desert.

Suddenly he stopped and said, "I have to check something on the bike. Can you get off for a second?" I climbed off, he lowered his foot onto the gas pedal, and took off. For a brief moment I thought he'd turn around and come back. But I stood there watching the taillight get smaller and hearing the noise of the motor fade until there was only silence around me. Silence and the occasional sound of wings, and something scurrying across the ground. I looked up at the dome of stars and then at the lights of the school buildings blinking far away from where I had been left. I remember the strange overwhelming feeling that I somehow belonged in this darkness, in the vastness all around me; for a moment I thought, if I just turned and walked into the night, got swallowed by it, no one would miss me. My bones would bleach in the sun like those of the dead cow I came across one day when I was riding my horse. What would it matter? I walked back to the lights of the school, the solitary sound of my own footsteps a familiar soundtrack to my life.

When I reflect back on that night, I linger on how at home I felt in all those wide miles of night. I think this is how we change—by looking at where we feel at home, what roads call out to us. They aren't always the best ones for us, they've just become familiar. It would take me a long time to realize that what's familiar is not always what's healthy. I also had to accept that that young girl, swallowed by darkness and resigned to its pull, remains in me still. But I choose to not be her, I choose to not let her intrude on who I am now. It's the best we can do with our past—move it aside and look beyond it, find beacons of light.

I didn't walk away from him after he abandoned me in the desert. I still believed we would be together. Whenever I hear about abused women remaining with their abuser, I understand why. I understand how something broke in them, how they can't wrench themselves away from the man who holds those broken pieces in his hands and claims that only he can mend them.

It was the following year—my senior year—when he and his family came to California for Christmas vacation. I invited them to our home, believing naively that all anyone would see was my fondness for the whole family. But you, Mom, were more astute than I gave you credit for. Much later, I would find out that you saw everything that day and chose not to say anything. More than a year would pass before we talked about it—about him. By then I was ragged and worn down, feeling older than any nineteen-year-old should.

I chose Northwestern University in Evanston, Illinois, because it was closer to him. He and his family had moved back to the Midwest. He was then teaching at a small college, and we would write letters, speak sometimes on the phone. I flew there and visited for a couple of days, sleeping on the couch in their living room. If his wife suspected anything, she never let on. He took me with him to his classes and on the drive back we pulled into a cemetery and made out in the car. He had commanded my world for several years by this point and I couldn't see beyond the boundaries of his dominance. We talked about him coming to Evanston on a weekend and us finally consummating our relationship. We even set a date and he told me when he would get into town, sometime after dark. I sat up until long after midnight waiting for his call, which of course never came. Nor did he call the next day, or the next. I had finally had enough. I left him without telling him I was leaving, but that didn't matter. I carried with me three years of wasted dreams; I carried with me a girl who had surrendered herself to a charismatic man many years older than she, who glossed over the humiliations, the lies, the false promises, and who bore the bruises of it all.

Mom, you had plans to come to New York shortly after that, and I asked if I could meet you there, stay with you for a couple of days. I don't know if you were surprised by my request, since it didn't quite fit with our usually strained relationship, but you quickly said yes. I had never been to Manhattan. I was enthralled with the city—with its hum of life and its spiraling architecture, with people filling the sidewalks and the weather changing quickly. You were staying at the Waldorf Astoria and had gotten a suite so I could stay with you. That's when the story of my last three years came out.

A light rain was falling outside the windows when we sat down to talk. It was afternoon, and earlier that day the skies had been clear. Then a storm moved in; it seemed somehow appropriate for what I was about to tell you. The city rumbled far below us, rain streaked the windows behind me, and I remember shivering a little as I began to tell you about my English teacher and the last few years of my life. I saw the expression in your eyes before you said anything.

"I've known for a while," you said. "I knew when they visited that Christmas."

"How did you know?" I asked.

"I just did."

I asked you why you didn't say anything for all this time, and you told me that you didn't think I'd listen to you, so you decided to let it play out and hopefully it would end sooner rather than later. You also said that you weren't going to tell Dad. "He'd be so upset, so angry," you said. You asked me questions, one of them being, "Have you made love?" and I answered you honestly. But I never told you about that night in the desert. I also never told you that I'd lost my virginity to someone else, hoping that the man I was in love with would then become my lover.

We went to a Broadway play that night. I'm pretty sure it was the musical *No, No, Nanette*, but I wasn't really paying attention to the play. I was caught up in a whirlwind of emotion. You had shown up for me as a mother who cared, who hurt for me, who wasn't judging me but was supportive. All of that felt so new and so welcome. I remember thinking that maybe the past few years of drama and foolish fantasies were worth it if they brought me here, to this moment, this feeling of safety.

It wouldn't last—nothing tender between us ever did—but I thought about those two days in New York for many years to come, wondering why we couldn't have remained like that.

◄–◄–►►

I NEVER FELT COMFORTABLE being the governor's daughter. Leaving Northwestern and returning to California to go to USC put me right at the center of things. I would sometimes drive past anti-Reagan demonstrations, and there was that one night when the two of you wouldn't let me leave the house and return to my dorm room because there was some kind of threat, but no one would explain to me what it was. Honestly, did neither of you ever understand that it's worse when you don't talk about things openly? This family turned secrecy into an art form.

America had now officially become part of our family, at least as far as I was concerned, and it loomed as the most important member. I felt pushed aside not only by the state of California, but by an entire country. I had no doubt, Dad, that you would ascend to a higher office, and I was haunted by all I believed that meant. Not only more distance between us, but the inherent dangers. I reflected often on President Kennedy's assassination, those long days off from school when the footage kept being replayed on television and the whole nation was in shock; Jackie's bloodstained suit, the image of her crawling toward the back of the car, the news story that the president's head was all but blown off. I had the same premonition as I'd had years earlier—a bullet would at some point find you.

We no longer spent weeks of the summer by the sea. I don't know if it was because of security concerns, or the logistics of having security personnel posted at a rented beach house, but those times were irretrievably gone. I missed the sea, and I missed the fragile peace it brought to our family. In the governor years, summers were mostly spent in Sacramento. I knew no one there, it was hot and dry and miles from the ocean. I'm not sure if the two of you ever figured it out, but my remedy for this misery was to stay stoned most of the time (I brought an adequate supply of pot with me from Los Angeles) and spend long hours in the pool. I was like a stoned Dustin Hoffman in *The Graduate*, just hanging out under the water. My other activity, which you did know about, was to drive up to Folsom Prison and go shopping in the gift shop there. I'm not sure exactly how this came about, but I think it had something to do with my fondness for Johnny Cash's album that he made at Folsom.

You don't know everything about those trips, though. Since I had my driver's license but did not have a car, I was allowed to borrow one of the state cars—a very unhip Lincoln Continental with some kind of radio system up front that I was told not to touch. So, I'd hit the road in a car that belonged to the governor's detail, get out of the city onto the open highway, and light up a joint. By the time I got to the prison, I was suitably stoned,

I had aired out the car by driving fast with all the windows down, and I was ready for my shopping spree. I was fascinated by the gift shop, and not just because I was stoned. Trustees manned the counter and there was a glass window behind them so they could be supervised. I longed to ask them what they had done to end up in prison, but sensibly I didn't. The aisles were full of handmade items that the prisoners had crafted—paintings, some of them dark and haunted, some dreamy and light-filled. There were intricately made things like dolls with movable parts, and puppets. On one trip I saw a stagecoach with a tiny carved gun rack that moved, wheels that turned, and a wagon cover made of white silk. The detail was amazing. I bought it and saved it until Christmas, when I presented it to the two of you as your gift. I truly thought you'd be impressed, Dad. I'd seen some of the western movies you'd done as a young actor, and when you were hosting *Death Valley Days*, we did a commercial together for Borax, with you dressed in a western getup. I thought it was something you would display and appreciate for its attention to detail, and for the story of a prisoner spending hours of his incarceration making it. But I never saw it again after I gave it to you.

One thing you might recall is an evening at the

dinner table when I was describing the gift shop to you both, and I mentioned that I was curious what crimes the trustees behind the counter had committed. Dad, you jumped right in and said, "You know, many of them are not there for violent crimes, but are there because of crimes of passion. Many of them killed their wives."

I thought Mom was going to choke on her food. She was horrified that you didn't see that as a violent crime, that you minimized it. Then you tried to backtrack and edit what you'd said. It was the closest thing to a squabble I'd ever seen between the two of you, and I loved it. It made you very real to me.

⤙⤚

I ENTERED USC as the governor's daughter in name only. I was the rebellious child, the wannabe hippie, so it wasn't like anyone wanted me at official events or asked me to play the role of governor's daughter, whatever that might mean. All I had ever wanted to do was be a writer, ever since I was that small girl at the edge of the playground, her nose buried in a book. So, I didn't particularly care if I graduated college. I chose mostly creative writing courses, some history classes, but I was uninterested in fulfilling the requirements of a college degree.

Someone—probably a professor—told me that I should have a backup career in case I couldn't support myself as a writer. By which they meant, something with a degree. Illogically, I decided that acting would be my backup. I plunged into the drama department, got small parts in a few plays, and I let the two of you think that I was following in your footsteps—that acting must be in my genes. When, in truth, acting was just my not-well-thought-out notion of a backup job in case writing wouldn't pay the bills. The two of you came to one play, in which I sang a duet and played guitar, and I was so nervous with you in the audience, I was shocked that I could get through it. I remember how unfamiliar it was, having the two of you there watching me; I was grateful that you came, but it felt like someone else's movie.

It was in those years, with the name Reagan sparking assumptions in whomever I met, that I decided I would change my last name. I simply wanted a moment of respite, so that someone who was just meeting me could perhaps see me as my own person, not merely as an appendage of a political figure about whom they already had opinions. I gave a lot of thought to this because I didn't want to hurt your feelings, Dad. I didn't want you to think that I was ashamed of bearing your name; I desperately wanted you to understand my reasons. When I said I needed to talk to the two of you about something, we sat in front of the blazing fireplace and I explained as carefully as I could why I wanted to have a name that felt like my own, and then I told you what I had decided the name should be. My calculation was that if I chose your maiden name, Mom—Davis—it would still be a family name, and the chances were good that I wouldn't offend anyone or get in trouble. I didn't know if it would work, since trouble was what I always seemed to get myself into. But, amazingly, it did. Both of you understood my reasons, and the fact that I was choosing another family name made the whole thing palatable.

Many years later, someone suggested to me that there were complicated psychological reasons why I chose your maiden name, Mom, that what was really at play was an attempt to get closer to the parent with whom I always clashed. For a moment I almost bought into that theory—that I was somehow groveling for acceptance and there was deep significance in my choice of the name Davis. But the truth is, I just didn't want anyone to get mad at me.

So, I left college as Patti Davis before my senior year, with "writer" as my goal, knowing that I'd somehow have to pay bills and thinking that getting some acting jobs would cover that. This was one of those long stretches of time when we had very little contact. I was working at a restaurant as a hostess, living with a roommate in a small apartment. Our history is dotted with so many separations, I don't even remember the reason for this one, or if there was a reason. I know we checked in with each other on birthdays, your anniversary, and I joined you for Christmas. But distance always seemed to whistle between us.

I wonder if either of you knew that shortly before Dad announced he was running for president in the 1976 election, an FBI agent showed up at my apartment building. Since neither of you were ever there, let me set the scene. It was a two-story, six-unit building in Santa Monica, all of us were in our twenties, and all of us did drugs. We shared drugs too; it was a very communal, friendly place. Since I worked at night in a restaurant I was often home during the day, and one day I saw a straitlaced man in a business suit walk past my window. This was a bit concerning, since the smell of pot smoke was a permanent reality at our building, and he did not look like he was coming to get stoned. I heard him knock on my neighbor's door, who also didn't have a nine-to-five job (actually, I don't think he had a job at all), and then I heard voices, but I couldn't make out what they were saying.

The man then went upstairs, and I again heard him knock on a door. Again, I heard voices. He never came to my door. It turns out he identified himself to my neighbors as an FBI agent who was there to ask questions about me. Questions like: Is there anything that might come out about Patti in a campaign that would embarrass Governor Reagan? Is she doing anything illegal? My neighbors all said no, and while I appreciated that they were trying to be protective, I was a little upset. It seemed like there might have been a slim chance, Dad, that you wouldn't have run for president if you were concerned that your hippie, drug-taking daughter might be exposed and become an embarrassment. Even though drug-taking hippies were fairly commonplace in those years, it probably wouldn't have played well in the political arena. I had never become comfortable with being the governor's daughter, and the idea of being a president's daughter terrified me.

I was still living in that building when I met and fell in love with a member of one of the most popular rock groups in the country, the Eagles. Bernie

Leadon and I met in a music store on a summer afternoon. He had no idea at first who my parents were. We tumbled into each other's lives, falling in love quickly and deeply. It never occurred to me to share with either of you how happy I was, how I felt that I'd found the love of my life; it's only now that I reflect on that omission. Our family's version of normal was that we didn't share in each other's highs and lows. When I was at USC, I was crossing the street one afternoon and got hit by a motorcycle. I was pretty banged up, I separated the cartilage on a rib, which was quite painful, but I never considered telling either of you about it. When Maureen was so abused by her husband that she had to escape and hide out at a YWCA, she never told you until years later when she wrote about it in a book. So, when I fell in love, there was never a thought of telling you about it. I've reflected on this in the years since as I've watched friends be so happy for their kids when they find happiness and love; the weight of all we missed out on takes my breath away. I wonder if you were ever curious about what was going on in your children's lives. Were there ever late-night conversations about us when you realized how little you knew?

I did tell you that Bernie had decided to use a song of mine, which he helped finish—"I Wish

You Peace"—on the upcoming Eagles album, and I remember you both seemed impressed by that. But then, when I moved in with him, you told me I was "living in sin." Suddenly there we were again in another ice age. We had very little contact for the next four years when Bernie and I were together. One year, I called Loyal to wish him happy birthday; he told me derisively that I was an embarrassment to the family, and then hung up on me. I have to say, while it wasn't at all amusing to me at the time, it is now. Mom, you were two months pregnant with me when you and Dad got married in a hurry—an out-of-wedlock pregnancy in the fifties being regarded as a sin—yet I was banished for living with the man I loved. The illogic is rather glaring. During those years, you ran for president, Dad, and lost the nomination. I remember standing in the kitchen of our canyon home hearing the news and feeling guilty that I felt so relieved. I'd had nightmares about Secret Service agents hiking up our steep mountain driveway to take over my life.

Here is something I'm fairly certain you never found out about. One day I was at my friends' house on the beach, just down from the canyon, and Bernie called. "Your brother Ron is here," he said. I hadn't seen Ron in years. Mom, you had made it clear that he was not to associate with me.

So, I had no idea how he could have found me. It turns out he looked up Bernie's name in the county recorder's office where they keep property titles, got our address, and headed into the canyon, stopping a few people along the way to ask where our street was, since it really wasn't much of a street, more like a paved trail.

When I walked into the house and saw him, I was struck by how tall and confident he was. He was both a stranger and achingly familiar. He spent the afternoon with us, we hiked up the hill in back of our house, and I fixed us an early dinner, most of which I picked from our vegetable garden. We did our best to get to know each other, but a lifetime of absence is like an undertow you can't fight. It will pull you out to foreign seas and leave you stranded there. We made no plans to see each other again and it would be years before we did. I will never understand, Mom, what the value was in fragmenting a family; decades later, the price you paid was steep when Dad was stolen away by Alzheimer's and you had no idea how to reach out to any of us.

The in-between time . . .

Dad, after you lost the Republican nomination in 1976, there were a few years when you held no office and weren't running for anything. It's probably not an accident that we got a bit closer during that time. Also, during that time Bernie and I broke up, both of us being somewhat immature in our own ways. I rented a small, funky, unheated house just down the hill from him, and I let you know that I had a new address. That launched a tentative reconciliation, and two visits to my new home. Here is what you don't know about my life at that time. When Bernie and I were together I had discovered gardening and quickly saw that I had a talent for it. I grew vegetables, strawberries, herbs, rotated crops seasonally. Then I tried my hand at growing pot and realized I had a talent for that too.

Ironically, Dad, you'd have appreciated the intricacy of growing pot, if you could have gotten past your judgment of the plant itself. You were always marveling at nature, once showing me some leaves in the woods at the ranch that, if wetted, turned soapy. Marijuana plants are male and female. In order to get the best pot—seedless, known as sinsemilla—the male plants have to be removed at just the right time. I wanted a few seeds for next year's crop, but I didn't want the entire female plant to be pollinated. So, at a certain point in the plants' maturity, I'd have to check multiple times a day and be right on top of it after I saw that a few buds had been pollinated. Then I had to quickly remove the male plants. I really think you'd have marveled at how detailed the whole growing process was. Someone advised me that removing the male plants too early could be a problem, not just because you'd have no seeds at all, but because the female plant wants so badly to be pollinated that it will turn hermaphrodite and pollinate itself. I've never independently verified this, and it's possible that the person giving me this tip was completely stoned, so I don't know if it's true. But it is a colorful detail. When I moved to my little cabin, I didn't have room to grow all the crops I had been raising. But I cleared a space on the side of the mountain for my pot plants.

Mom, you were the first to visit me there—you came for lunch one afternoon in the fall. It happened to be harvest time for marijuana. I had just taken the plants out of the ground and had hung them upside down from hooks in a small pantry room off the kitchen. That's what you do to make sure all the resin gets into the leaves and buds. Obviously, I couldn't let you see them. So, I carefully transported them to my neighbor's house and asked that they try to place them upside down for a couple of hours while you were visiting. As I showed you around my home, you peeked into the pantry, looked up at the ceiling, and said, "Why are all those hooks up there?"

Thinking quickly, I said, "The previous tenants were very tall and they used those as cup hooks. They could just reach up and get their coffee cups in the morning."

You seemed to buy it and didn't comment any further.

Then came the second visit, with both of you. Bravely, I'd invited the two of you to dinner. I can't recall exactly what month it was, but in marijuana time, my plants were tall and happily growing in my mountainside garden. It would be dark by the time you got there, so I wasn't worried about you seeing them. I was more worried about you falling down the long flight of wooden steps that went from the road to my house. There was only one light in the middle of the stairs—a tall gas lantern that I had to light with a match. I did suggest that you might want to bring a flashlight. So, after dinner, we were sitting by the fireplace, which was my only source of heat, and, Dad, you began talking about the canyon where I was living—specifically, that there were plans in place for law enforcement to start flying helicopters over the area because they'd gotten word that many people in the canyon were growing pot. I kept a straight face somehow, and tried to get a timeline out of you, but you were a bit fuzzy on that detail. I wasn't worried about a helicopter spying my plants. I'd had a friend who was a helicopter pilot in Vietnam look at where my plants were and he'd assured me that their location on the hillside made it basically impossible for someone in a helicopter to see them unless it swooped down and hovered really low, which was unlikely, but I knew several other growers in the canyon. The next day, I called all of them and reported what you'd told me. They all rushed to conceal their plants with lattice, potted trees, tents, and one guy later said to me, "Hey, Patti, thank your Dad for tipping us off, okay? That saved our asses!" I was going to point out to him that probably wouldn't be a good idea, but I decided to let it slide. The irony is, when you ran for president again in 1980, it's possible that a handful of pot growers voted for you.

The White House awaits . . .

Even though my fear that you would be president was still gnawing at me when you declared your candidacy for the 1980 election, I was really trying to be a good daughter during this time. I'd always been the bad girl, but I was getting tired of that role, so I decided to do my best to adapt, even though I had no clue what I was adapting to. I quit doing drugs, I quit growing pot, although that was dictated by my move out of the canyon and into the city. I tried to dress more stylishly. But I did have strong beliefs about what was going on in the country. I'd gone to a number of anti-nuclear events and meetings by that time, and I was passionate in my view that nuclear proliferation was putting the entire planet in jeopardy. Before you were elected president, Dad, no one really noticed or cared that I was part of this movement. I was just another attendee at crowded events listening to speakers like Daniel Ellsberg and Dr. Helen Caldicott (whose organization would go on to win a Nobel Peace Prize in 1985). Once you were elected, though, everyone knew I was part of that movement.

On one long, sleepless night in late 1980, the time between your election and the inauguration, I decided to look past all the pending inconveniences in my life (I knew the Secret Service were on their way to me) and think instead about the fact that I could help draw attention to an issue I cared deeply about. The anti-nuclear movement in the 1980s was significant, and it stood in opposition to your agenda of a nuclear buildup. But a spotlight I hadn't sought was suddenly on me too, and I earnestly, albeit naively, thought I could use that exposure to make a difference. As much as I did not want to be the president's daughter, I convinced myself that I could use that position to do some good. But before I could realize what my plan was going to get me into, there were some inconveniences I had to confront.

Two Secret Service agents arrived at my small Santa Monica apartment one afternoon after calling me and telling me they would be coming to see me. They were dressed casually, in khakis and long-sleeved shirts, but their earpieces gave them away. Sitting in my living room, they informed me that they would be with me 24/7, 365 days of the year. The detail leader, who was trying to coat the bad news with some humor, said, "Basically, we're here to ruin your life." While I appreciated his attempt at humor, I did indeed feel like my life was ruined. I was twenty-eight and single: How was I going to date? How would I ever find a relationship with heavily armed men following me everywhere?

"And your code name is going to be Ribbon," the agent said.

"You mean I'm not Patti anymore?"

"Well, in your private life, of course you are," he said. "But when we're on our radios we have to call you by your code name—Ribbon."

"What private life?" I asked. No one had an answer for that one.

Ron, Michael, and Maureen were all being visited by agents, were all getting their code names and a rundown of what the next four years of their lives would be like. In most other families, siblings would be on the phone with each other or hanging out together commiserating about this unfamiliar intrusion. I don't think it ever occurred to any of us to reach out to each other. We were so accustomed to our separate lives that sharing even an abnormal experience like this didn't dawn on us. Many years later I heard that a Secret Service agent said the Reagans never had much to do with each other, that we hardly ever got together.

And the last thing any of us would have done was talk to the two of you about how our lives were being reconfigured. Your shadow, Dad, officially grew in 1980 to encompass the country and much of the world. It swept over us too—enveloping us, trapping us, yet in the tent of that shadow none of your children could ever find who we needed you to be.

By the time the January inauguration was closing in, my detail of Secret Service agents had become familiar with me, although that wasn't always a good thing. They had implored me not to drive my own car and always ride with them, to which I had replied, "That is not going to happen." This meant I frequently lost them in traffic. I'd like to say it was accidental, and I didn't really mean to, but that would be a lie. I relished having a few minutes without them behind me in the rearview mirror.

Plans for the inauguration were under way, and while I'm sure that every president's inauguration is extremely choreographed, I'm guessing, Mom, that your hands were deep into this one. I was told that a designer would be loaning me a dress, and that an escort would be assigned to me for the night of the inaugural balls. (I didn't know until then that there were multiple balls.) As I said, I was trying to be a good girl, so I raised no objections. While I understood that since there was no man in my life, and you were afraid if, left to my own devices, I'd bring a drug dealer or a left-wing radical to escort me, recruiting your friend's son whom I hadn't seen since I was eight was a little strange. I'm sure it was odd for him too—I felt really sorry for him being dragged into an inaugural ball with a woman he didn't know.

When the dress arrived, I felt like someone had lassoed me—the ropes were tightening and there was nothing I could do about it. First of all, the dress was red. I hate the color red. And it had ruffles down the front; the last time I had worn ruffles was when I was a toddler. Putting it on, I looked like I should be in a small booth on a pier giving tarot card readings. Honestly, Mom, I thought it was a nefarious plot on your part to make me utterly miserable.

Then came the night of the inaugural balls. We had all gone to the White House following the swearing in and the parade. I was staying in Lincoln's Bedroom, which I did quite like, especially since I'd read that his ghost had occasionally been spied floating down the hallways. I put on the dress I hated and the high heels, which I also hated, and then someone knocked on the door and said I had to go see the hairdresser. I followed her into a dressing room area that looked like a beauty parlor and was told she was going to put my hair up.

That was a bridge too far, and I decided to speak up. "I don't want my hair put up," I told her.

She looked at me like I was insane. "You have to. You can't wear your hair loose like *that*."

I wondered if there was some list of rules about being in the White House and "no long hair" was one of them. I acquiesced and let her install my hair on top of my head. There is a formal family photo of the Reagans on inauguration night. I'm easy to spot. I'm the miserable one in the frilly red dress with a faint, forced smile and the severe Victorian updo, hunched over like she wants to disappear. But, Mom and Dad, you looked regal and happy, so I hope whoever sees that photo will just focus on that.

My assignment was to go to several balls with my escort, the guy who was a complete stranger to me. Playing on the swings together at eight years old doesn't really count as having a history together. We got to the first ball, the two of us and several of my Secret Service agents. We were led onto a stage where two metal folding chairs had been placed. Below and beyond the stage was a sea of people, crammed together, staring up at the chairs. It didn't look like a ball, it looked like those photos of people pressed together to watch a hanging. I will admit to you now, Mom and Dad, that I said to my Secret Service agents, "Are you fucking kidding me? This looks like an execution."

They shrugged, tried to stifle a laugh, and said, "You have to go out there." Then they dragged out two more chairs and placed them behind us, I guess in case the crowd rushed the stage, although I have no idea what they would have done. We sat there for what seemed like an eternity. Just sat there, as people pressed against the stage, took photos, waved at us. I'm claustrophobic, as you are, Dad, so you might understand when I say that even though I wasn't in that crowd, watching them all pressed together was giving me a panic attack. I turned around to my agents and hissed, "Get me the hell out of here!"

I guess they saw my panic and so they let us get up and then took us backstage. Lou Rawls was supposed to perform later, and someone said maybe we should go meet him. We made our way back to his dressing room. He was very charming, but I was still tied up in knots from the whole stage ordeal. Honestly, I was really regretting that I'd quit doing drugs and I thought maybe he might have some, but I didn't have the nerve to ask.

I did not go to the other balls I was supposed to go to. We dropped my escort at his hotel and I returned to Lincoln's Bedroom, tried to coax his ghost out to keep me company, but it didn't work. Much later that night, Dad, I heard your footsteps coming down the hall. I was pretty sure they weren't Lincoln's. You wanted to know why I hadn't gone to the other inaugural balls, and I lied and said I wasn't feeling well, that I had an upset stomach. Then you said something that I kept like a treasure for years. You said, "I know this is hard on all of you, Patti, and I'm sorry. I didn't want to complicate your life, but I had to do this. I really believe I can make a difference."

Somehow, I knew that I would never hear those words again, so I held them like diamonds in the palm of my hand.

I wish now, Dad, that I had tried to explain to you that I too wanted to make a difference. While I was uncomfortable with the sudden glare of a spotlight on me, I thought I could use it to do something significant in the world. I never attempted to have that conversation with you and, truthfully, it probably wouldn't have changed anything. But I would feel now as if I'd handled things better, rather than just going out and raising my voice about an issue we disagreed on, the predominance of nuclear weapons.

Before some of the rallies I spoke at, before I managed to enrage so many people with my activism, there was March 30, 1981, which almost ended everything. That gray, drizzly day when shots rang out and bodies fell around you, when you were shoved into the limousine, no one knowing at first that you had been hit until you coughed up bright red blood. John Hinckley shot three people out of the way just to get to you. The bullet fragmented inside you as it was meant to do—Hinckley having deliberately chosen that ammunition. It's a pity that, later, the jury that found him not guilty by reason of insanity didn't see his choices as proof of his chilling sanity when planning and carrying out his attack.

We never talked about what the rest of us were doing when we found out about the assassination attempt. No one ever asked, and I guess it seemed selfish to offer up our own experiences. But I want to tell you now where I was and how that awful day unfolded, hours crawling by not knowing if you would live, or even if you had already died and the news was being withheld.

I had started to see a therapist who worked out of his home, in a detached office space, very near to where I was living in Santa Monica. That's where I was when one of my Secret Service agents burst through the door. At first I was angry, thinking, Now they're even intruding on my therapy sessions? But his face was drained of blood and his eyes were full of alarm. "Patti, there's been a shooting," he said. He didn't need to tell me it was you, Dad, although he did. The agents only knew what was on the news—that you had been rushed to the hospital, walking through the door before collapsing, that three other men had been shot. Briefly, it was announced that James Brady had been killed, then that was corrected. The agents wouldn't let me drive my own car home, it had to stay in my therapist's driveway, nor would they let me rush to the airport and get on a plane. They told me they had to consider a worst-case-scenario, that perhaps the whole family was targeted. While they worked on how to get me back to Washington, the hours moved slowly, excruciatingly. I had the news on constantly, I knew you were in surgery, but in those years before cell phones I knew little else. It was so normal for this family to not communicate with one another that I actually never gave any thought to calling Michael or Maureen, and I had no idea where Ron was. I tried reaching Mom at the hospital via a number that the Secret Service gave me, but I was told she couldn't come to the phone. Finally, late in the afternoon, my agents said they had secured a military transport plane for me, Michael, and Maureen. As we sped away from my apartment, reporters who had been staked out in front started running after the car.

When we got to the airfield, Maureen was there with her husband, Dennis, Michael was there with his wife, Colleen, and I was by myself. Only Michael and Colleen came over to me. Maureen ignored me, which had become standard practice. I learned that Ron had been in another state—somewhere in the middle of the country—with the Joffrey Ballet, and his agents had gotten a plane to bring him to Washington. Military planes are loud and cavernous. They gave us headsets to block out the noise, brought us boxed lunches, and we flew east into night that had already fallen. At one point, Michael came over and sat beside me; just having another person that close made me burst into tears and I cried on his shoulder. "What if he dies?" I asked him. "Then we'll never have a chance of getting to know him." I don't remember Michael's response; I think he just nodded sadly, tears poised in his eyes.

We got to the White House sometime after two a.m. I slept a little, but was racked by nightmares, and then around dawn I got up and peeked into the bedroom where you should have been, Dad, but only Mom was there, lying alone, clutching one of your shirts. She said that she needed your scent beside her, she needed to hold on to something of yours.

That day exists in fragments in my memory. One piece that remains vividly clear is walking into your hospital room. You were lying back but someone had tilted the hospital bed up a bit and I was struck first by how pale you were and how sharply blue your eyes were against your skin. Then I was struck by something else. There is no other way of describing it—I saw a light around you, and I was certain you had died—maybe just for a moment, an instant—and come back. No one has ever spoken about your vital signs plummeting at any point, but I believed then and still believe that it happened. A story I heard later gave credence to my belief. You woke up in intensive care after the surgery and looked at the doctors standing around your bed. You were intubated and couldn't talk, so they gave you pen and paper. You wrote, "I'm alive, aren't I?" The interesting thing is you later described seeing people in white standing around you. Doctors in intensive care are in scrubs. No one is wearing white. But that's how you remembered it, or maybe that's what you saw earlier if I'm right and you did cross over and then return.

I didn't know until much later that while you were in intensive care, Tip O'Neill, the Democrat speaker of the House with whom you had many disagreements, came to your bedside, knelt down, and recited the Twenty-Third Psalm. He spoke gently to you and prayed for your recovery. We are so far away from that time now, Dad—from opposing political figures letting go of their politics and choosing humanity and compassion instead. In the midst of me writing this, Nancy Pelosi's husband was violently attacked in his home by a man who was after her, and there are Republicans making jokes about the attack that nearly killed this eighty-two-year-old man. None of them are kneeling in prayer for him.

After your ten-day hospitalization, I came back to Washington to be there when you were released. Mom and I rode together to the hospital and came into a small room crowded with Secret Service agents. It was the first time I saw the scar from the surgery that had saved your life, a scar that extended from your clavicle down to your abdomen. I thought of the surgeons opening you up and searching desperately for the bullet fragments that ended up dangerously close to your heart. You were still pale, weak, as they strapped a bulletproof vest on you. It was interesting that once the vest was on, it gave you more size, made you look a bit more robust, and you stood up taller, sort of puffed yourself up to face the crowd that was waiting for you outside. Here is what I thought as we walked outside, me on one side of you, Mom on the other: The last time you walked out into a crowd, raised your arm to wave, a deranged man opened fire and you nearly died. Yet here you were, waving and smiling, refusing to be cowed by that memory. I think you had too much humility to see yourself as brave, but that morning I saw you as incredibly courageous.

I don't remember us ever speaking about the jury's decision in Hinckley's trial. He was sent to St. Elizabeths Hospital in Washington, D.C. Mom, you and I might have talked briefly about it—about the shock of the verdict, the wrongness of it all. But, Dad, I never brought it up with you and I never heard you mention it, although I'm sure you must have expressed yourself to someone. What is still stunning to me, even all these years later, is what Dan Rather said on his news broadcast the day after the verdict was handed down: "If John Hinckley has the will (and he has shown he is willful) and the way (and his family is rich) he will probably down the road ask to be released from St. Elizabeths on the grounds that he is no longer dangerous. And sooner or later, a panel of experts may nod and say yes." Prophetic words, because that is exactly what has happened.

In 2000, the first time Barry Levine, Hinckley's attorney, made a strong bid for more freedom for his client, I wrote a piece for *Time* magazine that got a lot of attention. Levine ended up withdrawing the request, but only temporarily. Dad, you had already been pirated away by Alzheimer's. You knew nothing about Hinckley's quest, or the many articles I would end up writing every time another bid was made. Eventually, I had nothing new to say. And now John Hinckley is completely free. 1981 was a long time ago, but there is really no timetable when it comes to gun violence. It's an event that never dulls, that never feels far away. It changes you forever, as more and more people in America are finding out these days.

Recovering from your wound took time, but you plunged right in and started building up your physique, especially your upper body, where you were shot. Mom, you and I were speaking every day on the phone, and you would tell me how Dad would go into the room upstairs in the White House that had been converted to a gym and he would lift weights every day. It was fascinating to me that he was building up layers of muscle over his wound, his scar, almost as if to say, "Nothing is going to hurt me like that again." I don't know if you were exaggerating, but you told me that you had to have new shirts made for him because the size of his chest and shoulders had increased with his weight lifting.

But nothing erases the memory of being shot. It's indelible. Dad, you said that you wouldn't go to church services because you were afraid you might be putting others at risk. And the protection around you increased quite visibly, including Secret Service agents upstairs in the White House living quarters, which had never happened before. Gun violence, when it rips into your life, has no time frame, no end point. You were confronted with the scar on your chest every day, a reminder of a gray March day when you almost died. There were scars inside too—emotional scars—even though I know you didn't want to acknowledge those.

It took some time for you to get behind gun control legislation—I don't know if your hesitation was due to political pressure or a stubborn streak within yourself—but you did come out in support of the Brady Bill in 1991. You wrote an op-ed in the *New York Times* in which you referenced the assassination attempt a decade earlier. "This nightmare might never have happened," you wrote, "if legislation that is before Congress now—the Brady Bill— had been law back in 1981."

John Hinckley is walking free now; he has no restrictions on him, nothing preventing him from seeking out his remaining two victims, or family members of the men he shot. Mom is gone, so are both Jim and Sarah Brady, but the rest of us whose lives were changed that day have to live with the knowledge that he is living an unrestricted life. I don't want him in my mind, my thoughts, but I have no choice in the matter. When someone fires a gun at you or someone you love, they have in that instant carved themselves into your life, and there isn't a damn thing you can do about it.

Mom, I don't recall how much time elapsed

between the shooting and the news stories that you were relying heavily on an astrologer. I know at some point you spoke about how frightened you were for Dad's safety and having someone predict good and bad times based on the stars was a comfort to you. I never understood why you had to defend yourself at all. Why was it controversial that you were speaking with an astrologer? I was in no position to give you advice, but if I'd been able to, I'd have told you to shrug it off and say, "So what?" And I'd have suggested that you tell the truth about your history with astrology. When I was young, you used to go to someone in Westwood who would do astrological readings for you. You'd come home and tell me about it sometimes, and you used to read me my horoscope from the newspaper each morning. I often think that what is deemed controversial can be dismantled by just confronting it with confidence, as in, "What's the problem here? So what if I think there is wisdom in the stars?"

It strikes me now that I spent a lot of time imagining conversations I wanted to have with you, Mom. When I was a child, I imagined sweet innocent exchanges like the ones I witnessed with my school friends and their mothers. When I got older, I imagined more substantive ones about what was going on in your life or mine. Fantasies that never materialized.

We got into a pattern of speaking on the phone every day after the shooting. At end of the day, I would always call you. But we never talked about the placement of the stars or the guidance one might seek from astrology. We never talked about your fears or how you lived with the threat of danger each and every day after Dad almost died. We avoided the deepest topics. Our pattern of speaking every day didn't last long, though. My activism in the anti-nuclear movement brought our conversations to a halt. In fact, pretty much the only communication we had was publicly, through the press. I spoke at the anti-nuclear rally at the Hollywood Bowl in June 1981—a short message about a peaceful world without nuclear weapons, without the threat of the planet being destroyed. But despite what I told reporters—that I had a friendly and respectful disagreement with my father—it was probably clear to everyone that I was lying. There was nothing friendly or respectful in our difference of opinions. Rather, there was a resentful chill around my activism.

I've thought so much over the years about my choices during that time—not so much my ideological choice, as I believed deeply in the cause I was speaking out on—but about the ways in which I spoke out. I was conspicuously out in front when it came to anti-nuclear events; it never occurred to me that I could have an influence with less in-your-face exposure. Looking back now, it seems logical to me that I could have had a quieter voice while still (hopefully) having an influence. It's so tempting to stand in the present moment as the person you have grown into and look back judgmentally at the person you once were—in another time, having fewer tools or inner resources. And when the choices you made were played out publicly, as everything in the Reagan family was, it adds another layer of weight to those long-ago actions. There is a saying, "You never get a second chance to make a first impression." The first impression I made on a very public stage was that I was an angry rebel, out to embarrass my father, when that wasn't at all my motivation. In fact, in every interview I went out of my way to say that I was not trying to attack Dad, or shame him, I simply disagreed with his nuclear policy. But that point didn't really make an impact.

The truth I have to live with now is that while I was appearing at rallies, talking about world peace, the only thing being communicated was that I was at war with my father.

Dad, there was a day deep into your Alzheimer's

when I sat beside you and apologized for my actions in the eighties, for the public impression I created, and later for an ill-thought-out autobiography that caused you and Mom embarrassment and pain. I told you I wished I had done things differently, and I particularly wished we could have discussed the nuclear issue more. I didn't expect you to answer me, but I believed so fervently that your soul heard everything, I didn't feel as if my words got lost in the quicksand of the disease. I was certain that deep inside your being, you heard me.

I do, however, look at all this through a broader lens at this point. There are some other aspects to the story besides my mistakes. There were occasions when we could have discussed the nuclear issue, when I would have been willing to, but I was dismissed, told repeatedly that I was simply being used by the anti-nuclear groups I was working with, and that we were all being used by the Soviets, which seemed more than a tad far-fetched. I still blame myself for a lot, but I've stepped back far enough to get a clearer picture of everyone's role. There is no other way to say it—you didn't want to sit down with me and hear my opinions or concerns. I was just an irritant that had to be dealt with.

I've thought too about the other reasons I got involved with such a controversial issue, why I walked out onto the battlefield and stayed there. I've thought about the girl who didn't think she mattered, who didn't believe she should even be taking up space on the earth, the girl who was told that God put everyone here for a reason but who was searching for hers. I was still the little girl who stayed awake all night on the train to Phoenix, staring out the window at the black night and the lights of far-off homes, wondering if the people in those houses felt like they belonged. And the eighteen-year-old, abandoned in the dark desert by a man she loved, who thought she might as well just vanish into the darkness. I was still the nineteen-year-old who sat in a small bathroom with the light from a streetlamp slanting through the window, holding a razor blade against the soft veins of her wrist—it would be so easy, just a little pressure. But there was always an ember in me—a longing to leave something behind, to make a difference. If the anti-nuclear groups I worked with were using me, I was using them too, but we were all being pushed by the same desire—to leave an imprint on this planet, to make it a better place with a more hopeful future.

All of that was in play when I approached you, Dad, with an offer to bring Dr. Helen Caldicott, the very well-known anti-nuclear activist, to the

White House for a discussion. I was thrilled when you agreed to the meeting, and what I didn't say at the time was that I had a bigger dream than just that one meeting. I wanted it to launch a series of meetings with other activists and scientists; I really believed this could bridge the yawning gap that existed so we could at least have an on-going dialogue. I also believed it would let people see you, Dad, as more open and willing to listen to other viewpoints—not an opinion that many had of you at the time.

So, when I arrived at the White House late that evening, having flown in from California, my heart sank when I read the handwritten note that you had left on the pillow in Lincoln's Bedroom. You said that you and Mom were out for the evening and you would see me the next day for our meeting, but you wanted to keep it private. You didn't want any media to know that you had met with Helen Caldicott. I remember the sinking feeling inside me. As I said, part of the point was to have it be public knowledge that you had agreed to the meeting, and hopefully to more that would follow. I sat in the dimly lit room staring at Lincoln's portrait, whispering to him—as I had before when I stayed there—that I felt beaten down again. I wondered if he had ever felt as if nothing he did mattered. As monumental a figure as he was, did he ever have moments when he feared that his voice might just echo back to him and then be buried in the canyons of time?

The next day, I met Helen for an early lunch and then we went to her hotel room. We got down on our knees and prayed for a constructive outcome to our meeting. When we both uttered, "Amen," I thought, the two of you had something in common—the belief in prayer, in turning things over to God and asking for His guidance. Maybe you weren't as far apart as you thought. But that moment of optimism and hope was short-lived.

The meeting was not scheduled for the Oval Office—by design, since you didn't want anyone to know about it. We were led to one of the little-used rooms in the White House, I can't recall now which one. You were about five minutes late and when you walked in, my heart sank. I knew it wasn't going to go well. I saw the look in your eyes—that impenetrable blue wall I'd seen before on other occasions. A look that said, "I have my mind made up and nothing you can say will make a difference." I spoke very little; I let Helen lead the charge. She was passionate but respectful, wanting very much to try to get you to consider the danger the world was in because of the proliferation of nuclear weapons, why a nuclear freeze was what we needed, to ensure the planet would survive. But that look in your eyes didn't waver. You were waiting for her to stop talking. When she paused, you immediately told her—us—that the Soviet Union was behind the nuclear freeze movement, that we were all being used by the Soviets, that this was a well-planned effort to undermine America's strength. At one point, Helen interrupted you, fearlessly, and said, "You got that from *Reader's Digest*." I think you said something about having gotten your information from other sources as well. We met for a little over an hour, with nothing to show for it. Helen and I walked down the wide hall of the White House, our footsteps echoing around us, as footsteps tend to do on the hard floors of the people's house, and she said, "I'm really scared now."

That night, I sat with you and Mom in the upstairs dining room—one of the tense meals that characterized so much of our family history. I ate little and drank too much wine, trying to drown the grief I felt over what I regarded as my failure. Mom, you said very little, which was unusual. Dad, you repeated your assertion that the entire nuclear freeze movement was being manipulated by the Soviets, and, honestly, by that point I had nothing else to say and no energy left. I went back into Lin-

coln's Bedroom that night and whispered my con-
fessions and concerns to him again. It seems so sad
to me now that I had more truthful and raw conversations with Lincoln's ghost than I was able to
have with you.

At this same time, a plague was sweeping
through the gay community. I had friends who dis-
appeared, locked themselves in their homes with
lesions or pneumonia. When I talked to them on
the phone there was someone else on the line—
Death whispered that it was coming for them.
Going to the hospital wasn't a great option. There
was so much confusion and misinformation about
how AIDS could be transmitted. Through touch?
Through saliva? Hospital personnel typically wore
hazmat suits when dealing with AIDS patients;
food trays were left outside the doors. And all
the while, Dad, your administration was doing
nothing. Saying nothing. I wanted to intervene, I
wanted to try to get through to you but, honestly,
I felt broken and useless after what had happened
with my efforts in the anti-nuclear movement.

I was shocked to learn that people in your
administration often made jokes about AIDS.
I know it isn't something you would have done,
or sanctioned, but it happened on your watch
and there is no way to circumvent that bit of his-

tory. There is audio of your press secretary, Larry Speakes, in an exchange with a reporter named Lester Kinsolving at a daily press briefing. Kinsolving asks Speakes about AIDS; he says it's being called the "gay plague," that people are dying. To great laughter Speakes responds, "I checked thoroughly with Dr. Ruge this morning and he's had no patients suffering from A-I-D-S or whatever it is." This is just one example documented in *When AIDS Was Funny*, a film by Scott Calonico.

I still don't believe at that point that I could have done anything, but I also am still haunted by the fact that I didn't try. Maybe I should have pushed past my own sense of defeat and tried to make some noise.

You finally intervened, Mom, but so much damage had been done by then, I'm not sure how much difference the pressure you exerted made. It was in May 1987 and Dad was going to give a speech at a fundraising dinner for the American Foundation for AIDS Research. By all accounts, it was you who wanted him to go to that dinner and speak. You also didn't want the ultra-conservative members of his administration to compose the speech, since they were in many ways responsible for his silence on the plague that was claiming so many thousands of lives. You brought in a speechwriter,

Landon Parvin, who had worked for you during Dad's first term. But even though he invoked your power and influence to push back against people like Pat Buchanan, the speech Dad ended up giving was watered down and way too mild to be consequential. He was booed at several intervals.

Years before that—I don't recall exactly when— you and I were speaking on the phone and you told me that a friend of yours had just died. You said it was hard getting older because you were now suffering through the deaths of so many friends. I told you that I was much younger and was losing just as many friends, if not more, to AIDS. You paused and said in a subdued voice, "I know." Of course you knew. You had many gay friends, you read the paper each morning, listened to the news every evening, so all I can do is wonder if you tried to get Dad to address the crisis earlier in his administration. My other memory about that phone conversation is that I pointed out to you that when Dad was shot and had to have a massive blood transfusion, he could easily have contracted AIDS. It was 1981—there was no screening process for HIV-tainted blood. It was quite possible that he could have contracted HIV from that transfusion, given how much blood he received.

One of Dad's shortcomings was to trust other

people to tell him what he needed to know and to guide him along the best path possible. It was a naivete that, I assume, sprang from his own nature. He was a genuinely kind person who would never have tricked others to get what he wanted. But there were those around him who did exactly that, who led with their own anti-gay prejudices and did not want him to address an epidemic that was predominantly affecting homosexual men. Too willing to believe what he was being told, he didn't question those in his administration who told him that money was being spent on AIDS when, in fact, it wasn't. But you knew he had that tendency. I've always thought that's why you were so ferocious in your desire to protect him, influence him, steer him in the direction you thought best. Because you knew he could be led astray by people who parceled out the information they gave him. So, what happened with the AIDS crisis? Years passed before he addressed it. Thousands of people were dying horrible deaths.

There are times I imagine the two of us talking about Dad's willingness to believe others, even those he should have doubted. I conjure up a picture of us sitting peacefully together, talking affectionately about his foibles. But it's not a conversation we could have had. It's funny, after someone dies you find yourself imagining scenarios that would never have occurred when they were alive. In that unbounded land after death the wildest things seem possible. The truth is, it would have been too intimate a conversation for us to have, one focused on the man you drew boundary lines around, even keeping his children from getting too close.

The fact that there were people around him who had a clear-cut agenda when it came to AIDS (specifically, to not let him talk about it) doesn't mean he is blameless for the tragic silence coming from the White House in those years and the appalling lack of action. I have no doubt, Mom, that you were fully aware of this and that's why in 1987 you pushed so hard to have Dad speak at the AIDS fundraiser and why you insisted Landon Parvin write a speech that should have been given years earlier.

No matter how many different colors are on the palette of those years, no matter how I try and look at the anti-gay people in the administration and Dad's willingness to put blinders on and believe their lies, the truth can't be understated—an epidemic was ignored. People died, most of them gay men. Many of them took their own lives as the disease ravaged them. I lost people about whom I cared deeply; their gaunt faces and wide frightened eyes will stay with me forever. I understand why so many people can't forgive Dad for those years; it's a weight I will always bear.

Dad, another part of the heartbreak for me is when I hear people accuse you of having a prejudice against gays. I know without any doubt that this is not true. I grew up around a gay couple— Aunt Glesca and Aunt Emily, friends of Mom's who became friends of yours as well. I think they were a little older than you, and I remember Aunt Emily often wore shirtdresses like Donna Reed wore on her television show. In my mind, they were a married couple; even though no one actually said that. Everything about their lives looked like marriage. I visited them in the apartment they shared; they were always together, they even babysat for me and Ron, who was a toddler then, when you and Mom went to Hawaii. They slept in your bed. Nothing about this seemed strange to me. And you, Dad, were the one who explained to me that some men like other men, and some women like other women. I remember the conversation as if it just happened . . .

We were in the den one evening watching television; I was about eight or nine. A Rock Hudson/ Doris Day movie was on, and in one scene they kissed. I was sitting on the floor and you were in the armchair. I looked up at you and said, "That's weird." Intrigued, you asked me what I meant. I told you I didn't really know, it just looked weird to see the two of them kissing. You leaned down and gave me one of your serious looks, always a signal that I was going to learn something important.

"Well," you said, "that's because he doesn't really want to be kissing her. He would rather be kissing a man. Some men fall in love with other men. Some women fall in love with other women."

I think I mentioned Aunt Glesca and Aunt Emily then and you said something like, "Yes, like them."

I don't understand why you allowed people to be in your administration who believed that homosexuality was a sin, and even felt that AIDS was God's punishment against them. But I know you were not in that camp and it's painful to hear people suggest that you were. I keep stumbling over unknowns yet holding tight to the few truths I am certain of. Still, the blunders and neglect when it came to an epidemic that, by 1987, had taken the lives of more than forty thousand people in this country is a weight I can't lift off you no matter how many other truths I assemble. I search for kindness—any kindness—coming from the White House during the vast sweep of AIDS and I find only failure. The lifeguard who pulled seventy-seven people from the perilous waters of a river where they would surely have drowned stood by passively while thousands died from a fatal disease. That's not who you were, that was not your nature, yet that's what you did.

When Rock Hudson died from AIDS in 1985, even the most die-hard people in your administration couldn't turn your attention away from that. He had been a longtime friend, the two of you used to attend Screen Actors Guild meetings together, but he had hidden his illness from almost everyone, including you. It was the first time you publicly addressed the disease, but still the urgency that America needed to hear from you wasn't there. Many years later, I learned that after Hudson's death, you went to the White House physician, John Hutton, and asked him to tell you all about AIDS. After he did, you told him you had assumed it was like measles and would go away. According to Dr. Hutton, you said, "I always thought the world would end in a flash but this sounds much worse." You did make a call to Tip O'Neill after that and made it clear you wanted more funding for AIDS research, so some progress was made, but not enough.

One puzzling aspect of this is that your sense of timing, Dad, was usually spot-on. I don't know if it was instinctual or learned from your years as an actor, but your timing was impressive. It was part of what made you "the great communicator." Yet, with AIDS, you were late on everything. In 1987, you learned about Ryan White, the Indiana teen who contracted AIDS from a blood-clotting medication he took for his hemophilia, when Landon Parvin wanted you to mention him in the speech he was writing for you. But he was overruled by the ultra-conservative members of your administration, and you allowed that to happen. You were not typically passive about things, yet when it came to AIDS, you were. There was no mention of Ryan in that speech.

Ryan White was thirteen when he contracted HIV-AIDS. He was then forbidden to go to school, he was ostracized in his hometown of Kokomo, and he was given six months to live. Ryan fought back against all of it. He became an eloquent voice in the fight against AIDS and against the prejudice of those who dismissed it as a "gay disease." You could have joined with him while you were president, you could have stood beside him, yet you didn't meet with him until you were out of office, in 1990. Less than a month later, Ryan White died. You wrote an op-ed in the *Washington Post* about Ryan in which you said, "Nancy and I wish there had been a magic wand we could have waved that would have made it all go away." Your piece didn't go over well. A man named David Robinson wrote a response that began: "As a gay man who has been fighting AIDS for three years . . . I found Ronald Reagan's tribute to Ryan White one of the most infuriating and embittering things I've read in a long time." Robinson went on to say: "He may not have had a wand, but he had the next best thing: the presidency of the United States for the first 8 years of the AIDS epidemic."

I reach for possible explanations, complexities that might offer some counterpoint to the icy reality of the facts. But I grab on to nothing but air. Years ago, after you were gone, I thought it might be helpful if the Reagan Library addressed the AIDS crisis that sits so heavily on your legacy. There is basically nothing about it at the library. I wrote a lengthy email to the appropriate people there and suggested tackling the subject, maybe even having an event where it could be discussed, because ignoring it was not going to work in anyone's favor. I pointed out that keeping it in shadow, staying silent about that part of your history, only solidified the bitterness that many people have. I expressed my opinion that tackling the subject, having the courage to open the gates and let all viewpoints in, would benefit your legacy. I got a brief response of thank you, we'll look into it, but nothing was ever done. So, I am left with the tides of anger that I still encounter from other people. I'm left with my own observations and my own disappointment. And, as usual, I'm left with unanswered questions.

<del>-<-->-</del>

THERE IS ANOTHER REGRET that haunts me, which conversely is about something I wish I had praised you for. In 1987, you and Mikhail Gorbachev signed the agreement reducing nuclear weapons, yet I didn't congratulate you or express pride, and I should have. It was just so easy in this family to fall back into a stalemate of silence. It felt too much like home, so I kept going there, even though I longed for something different. Even though I knew that what you had done was historic. No other president, before or since, has done something so extraordinary—eliminating an entire class of nuclear weapons. And yet I said nothing to you . . . until you were ill and far away, many years later, and I whispered to you how proud I was of you for making the world safer. Do you know that Gorbachev came to your funeral service in Washington, D.C.? It was the first and only time I met him. We shook hands and his eyes were soft and sad; he looked lonely—his wife, Raisa, had passed away in 1999. In somewhat broken English, he told me that he missed you, and I fought back the tears that fell so easily in those days after your death. I think God puts people together on history's stage for an express purpose. Maybe they will fulfill that purpose, maybe they won't. The two of you did.

A white wedding . . .

I WAS HARDLY SURPRISED, Dad, when you won a second term in 1984. This time around, no one asked me to attend any inaugural balls, and I probably wouldn't have if I had been asked. My attention was elsewhere. I had fallen in love, and neither of you had met him or knew anything about him.

So, you were understandably surprised, Mom, when I told you that I was going to marry the man I had been dating—and had been living with for a while. I said I wanted a real wedding, white dress and all. I don't know what I expected, but the tone of your voice through the phone line chilled me. You said, "All right. Well, how do you plan to do that?" Paul was six years younger than me, a yoga instructor, and radiated a kind of clean innocence.

Dad, when you and I finally talked about it and I told you that he taught yoga, you at first mis-heard me and thought I said "yogurt." Perplexed, you asked how someone makes a living with yogurt. It was all very awkward. I've wondered over the years why I said I wanted a traditional wedding. It's not exactly my style, and Paul would have been content to just get married on the beach at twilight with a few friends as witnesses. When I told him I wanted a wedding with a white dress and my father walking me down the aisle, he looked at me as if he weren't sure who exactly he was marrying. At moments when I'm down on myself, I've wondered if my choice was spurred by some hidden agenda toward you, Mom. You didn't have a white wedding. Two months pregnant, you got married in a tiny out-of-the-way church, wearing an austere gray suit with only William and Ardis Holden (his then-wife) as witnesses. Was I trying to one-up you? I've asked myself that several times and I've concluded that I wasn't. It's more likely that I was trying again to move away from always being the bad girl, the rebel. "Look," I was saying, "I can be a normal girl in a wedding dress, with bridesmaids, walking down the aisle toward the man I am marrying."

I wonder how the two of you would feel if you

knew that, at the Hotel Bel-Air, where Paul and I were married beside the pond, with swans floating past and lush ferns and shade trees surrounding us, there is now a large photo of me and Dad walking down the aisle. A number of friends have told me about it; it seems to be hanging in a very conspicuous place as guests walk into the dining room.

Two memories from that day stand in stark contrast to one another. The first is just before the ceremony, when I was in the hotel room standing in front of the mirror in my long white dress and veil. Several other people, including my bridesmaids, were there. You walked in, Dad, and you never even glanced at me. You started telling a story about something—some current event, perhaps. You were being the entertainer, the quick-witted performer, the GE host—it came so naturally to you. I remember feeling invisible. If I were the person then that I am now, it's possible I would have said something. Maybe, "Hey—it's my wedding day, I'm right here." But I said nothing, just curled in on myself, accustomed to the feeling of invisibility.

But then, after the ceremony, at the dinner, you stood up to give a toast. You talked about the tiny baby I once was, how my hand was swallowed by yours when you held it. You talked about time, how fast it moves, and how you had now given away my hand—a woman's hand—in marriage. As I listened to you, tears welled up in my eyes. The two halves of our relationship loomed over my wedding day— the girl who craved more of her father's attention, and the woman who grabbed on to her father's words, squeezing every tear out of them, who decided that the latter was what she would lean into and embrace.

Mom, this is difficult to say, but throughout the wedding planning, I felt as if you resented me for getting married, for having the wedding you never had. I'm sure that's why I started questioning myself, wondering if I'd chosen a traditional wedding just to get under your skin. But, truthfully, I'm not that conniving. After we were married, Paul and I saw you and Dad on holidays like Thanksgiving and Christmas, if we didn't travel to Montana to see his family, but there was no casual or frequent interaction between us. I've never known how to scale the walls you put up; at a certain point I had stopped trying.

I was speaking to Ron only occasionally, and on one of those occasions he told me that he had "signed off" from Secret Service protection. He'd researched it and discovered that, if the presidential offspring are not minors, it is possible to remove protection. I was elated. I had lived with a posse of heavily armed men following me for four years; now I was married to a man who I knew didn't like this intrusion. I decided I was going to follow in my brother's footsteps.

There is a procedure for this. You have to write a letter to the Secret Service. They then send it up the chain of command, and one of the higher-ups visits you for a serious and (he hopes) frightening conversation. I don't know how much the two of you ever knew about this, so I'll give you a brief synopsis of the conversation.

"You are putting yourself in grave danger by not having our protection. There are frequent kidnapping threats against members of the first family. We evaluate those all the time, and some of them are credible," intoned the high-ranking Secret Service agent.

I countered with, "Well, it seems to me if a kidnapper with any kind of intelligence looked at the Reagan family, he wouldn't say, 'Let's take Patti.' I mean, who would pay the ransom?"

The high-ranking Secret Service agent almost laughed but caught himself.

So, without my cadre of armed agents, Paul and I had a pretty simple life—almost normal. He taught yoga classes, I was helping to support us with my backup career—acting. I was doing small guest parts on some network shows, but all I really wanted to do was write. When I came up with an idea for a novel and got a publishing deal, I had unwittingly stepped into another quagmire.

◄◄—►►

HOMEFRONT, MY FIRST BOOK, was an innocuous and somewhat naive novel that ascribed to the basic literary rule of "write what you know." Like many writers, with some notable exceptions, I don't want anyone to go back and read my first book, for such books are about finding your voice, honing your skills, unearthing confidence in the mysterious relationship between your brain and words. I wrote about a family steeped in politics, in which the father was a governor with soaring presidential ambitions, a family in which a rebellious daughter was at odds with her father's politics. Familiar territory, but I made the daughter older than I was. She was an activist during the Vietnam War when I was still in high school. And the relationships in my quasi-fictional family were actually warmer than the relationships in our family. The mother and daughter had conversations, they even went shopping together.

None of that made any difference when the book

was published. I believed then, and still believe, that neither of you ever read the book. The media pounced on me because I had already solidified my image as the bad girl of the family. The novel was regarded as a slash-and-burn attack on the two of you. One journalist even voiced disgust that, in one scene, the mother was wearing a red suit. Mom, you called several people who were scheduled to interview me and asked them to cancel; they did. My publishers called me with the bad news and said they'd never quite seen anything like this. Dad, you injected a critical comment about the book in a press conference. The book did deserve criticism—for not being a very good book. But it didn't warrant the barrage of insults that came my way. It certainly didn't warrant the death threats that came my way.

When I had finished the novel, I was proud of it. I thought it was a good story and, as a novice writer, I felt I had successfully straddled the line between fiction and real life. But as soon as it was published, not a shred of my pride remained. I felt like I was at the bottom of a junk pile that had been tossed on top of me, and I was trying to claw my way out from under it. I wonder, if you had actually read the book, would you have seen it as the some-what innocuous story it was?

Years later, a journalist was interviewing me for a subsequent book—I believe my third or fourth by then—and she said, "I remember when your first book came out. Things were so brutal for you, I figured you would never write again."

I've thought of her words occasionally, and about the fact that it never occurred to me to stop writing. Truman Capote once said about himself that he had "something peasant-like and stubborn" in him and he was "in it till the end of the race." Looking back, I guess that's who I decided I was going to be. The irony, Dad, is I think I got that from you.

All this drama put a strain on my marriage, although it's possible that Paul and I were just never well suited for each other. He wanted a mellow life, teaching yoga and practicing his meditation. Being married to the president's daughter didn't exactly fit that recipe, and if you add in the built-in dramas of the Reagan family, a mellow life was not really attainable.

I suppose I could have chosen to write only happy novels where everyone got along, but instead, in 1992, when you were out of the White House, I wrote an autobiography. I have said in the past to you both, and will say again, that I regret writing that book. I was angry that I had been attacked for the piece of fiction that was my first book, so I thought, Fine—I might as well tell the truth. Then everyone can see how mild the family in my novel was. I was also driven by the fact that I have a rabid desire to tell the truth, since in our household truth was a movable object.

There was something else going on too. Partially influenced by my husband and his spiritual work, I had started working on how I viewed things internally, what lens I was looking through. I began focusing on forgiveness and trying to understand why people behave the way they do. I did bring much of that to my writing, but I was still in first grade when it came to a more spiritual way of thinking. Here is my take on my autobiography, the title of which I refuse to even mention: I emphasized that forgiveness is the answer to everything, but I was so new to that way of thinking, I then leapt to, but let me tell you everything I'm forgiving them for—in detail.

I learned an important lesson from writing that book, and from once again going through public backlash—I learned that while telling the truth is important, not every truth needs to be told in excruciating detail to the entire world. I think of this every time a famous person writes a memoir and says they wanted to put everything out there and hold nothing back. Something catches in me, some small voice whispers, "Uh-oh."

Saying goodbye . . .

BY THE TIME MY MARRIAGE ended around 1993, we were long into another arctic winter in our relationship. I don't even remember if I told the two of you that I was getting divorced. What followed was an empty, desperately bleak time when I stumbled into an abusive relationship that ultimately propelled me out of California to the East Coast, where I knew no one. Looking back, I see now that I had never before felt so lost in the vast emptiness of having no family to turn to. I don't say that to cast blame; it's simply a fact. I've wondered, Mom, if you ever felt anything like that in the years when Dad retreated into Alzheimer's. You had never opened yourself up to the embrace of a family. You had never tried to pull our family together, and by that time you had no idea how to do it. Did you ever lie awake at night and imagine what life might have been like if our family wasn't such a fractured mess? If, in the midst of grief and loss, you could have relied on a family that enveloped you with love?

I was scraping by in New York writing magazine pieces, finding my way in a city that can be overwhelming—it moves at lightning speed and you have to keep up or be swallowed by it. I was making friends, but I was also fighting tidal waves of depression, a persistent feeling that I was an utter failure in everything I did. We had no inter-action during that time. When I read in the news-paper, Mom, that you were coming to the city and would be appearing with Charlie Rose at the 92nd Street Y for an interview, I called your office staff and asked if I could arrange to see you. Then I bought tickets to the event for myself and two of my friends—a gay couple whom I had become very close to. I was given an appointment to see you in your hotel room the morning of your event.

You were staying at the Carlyle Hotel, at Mad-ison and Seventy-Sixth. I remember being let into your suite by a member of your staff and, despite the heat being cranked up and the wash of sun spilling through the windows, the chill emanating from you was palpable. It was late morning. You were still in your bathrobe, sitting beside a table with uneaten food on it, while I sat down in a pool of sunlight on the uncomfortable sofa. I don't remember now what words I used, but I do know that my purpose was to see if we could have some kind of relationship, if we could move past the resentments and all the things I had done wrong . . . maybe try being a family.

You seemed to soften a bit, then a little bit more

as we talked, and eventually you told me that Dad had been diagnosed with Alzheimer's. It wasn't the first time I had heard this, but before, it seemed more like a possibility, not an irrefutable fact. Ron had told me that a few years earlier when Dad fell off a horse and suffered a head injury, an MRI already showed signs of early dementia. But Ron wasn't supposed to tell anyone, you hadn't told Dad or, obviously, me, so it was another secret simmering just under the surface. But now, in the yellow sun-wash of a New York morning, sitting uncomfortably in a gilded hotel suite, it became real. I don't think I let it sink in until after that evening when I went to see you at the 92nd Street Y. I remember Charlie Rose, when I went backstage afterward, looking at me with a shocked expression on his face. I could almost hear the thoughts in his head: What is *she* doing here? This family never shows up for each other.

Dad, I want you to know something about getting the news of your diagnosis, something I didn't tell you even in those soft hours when you'd been stolen away by the disease and I would sit with you. I told you so many things, things I believed your soul could hear. But I didn't tell you about those barren months of 1994 when I was in such a dark tunnel I thought seriously and often about taking my life. As strange as it might sound, your Alzheimer's was the rope that kept me from drowning. I wanted to be there for you; I wanted to show up for whatever this mysterious disease was going to bring into your life, and whatever it was going to take from it. It was the second time you had saved my life, and you never knew about either time. You never knew about your nineteen-year-old daughter who pulled the razor blade back from her wrist because she heard your voice in her head telling her that God puts everyone here for a reason. I decided God's plan couldn't be for me to die in a small bathroom by my own hand, with the blue glow of a streetlamp shining through the winter-frosted window.

Now you were saving me again so many years later with the grace of your acceptance when fate targeted you with a disease that no one knows how to handle. I not only wanted to show up for you, hold your hand on the unpredictable journey, but I wanted to learn and grow by watching how you would deal with this thief called Alzheimer's— the thief who always gets the last word. I should have whispered, "Thank you," to you on one of those afternoons when I visited and we were alone. I should have told you that I was grateful to be here, grateful that your voice reverberated in my head, even though for much of my life I have felt unmoored. You had told me that God never leaves us alone, that He is always here, and by telling me that, you kept me here.

◄-◄-►-►

THE NEXT TEN YEARS of your illness changed so many things in my life, in our lives—more than I realized at the time. I treasured your softness, your gentleness; I sank into the blue distance of your eyes instead of resenting that distance, as I had for so many decades. I found in myself a confidence I hadn't felt before, trusting that in that blue space I would find pieces of you. And I did. I met the boy, the teenager, the lifeguard. I was no longer grasping for you to be the father I wanted you to be. I was, instead, content to know who you were as a person, all the puzzle pieces of you that had come together to form a man who stepped onto the world stage and became part of history. I finally let go of my rivalry with America, the player who had always commanded more of your attention, and became grateful for the concern that total strangers had for you.

My journey with you, Mom, was not as smooth, but then, when were things ever smooth between us? After flying back and forth between New York and California to see Dad as often as I could,

I was running out of money. I decided to move back to Los Angeles. I sold all my furniture, put a few things in a storage locker in New York, and arranged to stay in a spare bedroom at a friend's house. I didn't have enough money to rent anything, but I had started writing *The Long Goodbye,* so I had hopes for a publishing deal. I didn't tell you any of this, except that I was moving back. I don't even know how things got strained again between us that time around. There had been a few nice visits when you came to New York, but somehow everything turned brittle and cold again. So, I didn't tell you where I was living when I returned to Los Angeles, nor did you ask. For the first time in my life, I didn't spend time and energy wondering what I had done wrong this time, why you were angry with me again. My focus was on Dad and the disease that was whittling him away. I wanted to be fully present for that, and, to be honest, your displeasure with me, your coldness, was just a distraction. There was something liberating in adopting that attitude. I had the distinct and unfamiliar feeling that I was actually handling things like an adult. Interestingly, you apparently got tired of your wintry siege. For no obvious reason, you just started warming up again and we were able to talk about Dad and the challenges that faced us both.

It was not a smooth decade in terms of our interactions and our relationship. But the difference was, I had made a pledge to myself to not act from a place of wound. I didn't always get it right, but when I got it wrong, I owned it and corrected myself. I learned, if you were coming at me harshly, to simply withdraw and wait for the cold wave to pass. I realized, in those years of illness, how much of a hold you'd always had on my life. You could block out the sun, or you could let summer in, and I had to constantly remind myself that I had strength too. I had command over the seasons of my life, and I had the ability to hold firm and not be tossed from one weather system to another.

What I didn't have command over was Alzheimer's, and my acceptance of that had a profound effect on me. There is something illuminating about being in the presence of something huge—like a disease—that you can do nothing about. It forces you to think differently, to ask different questions. I began to constantly ask, What can I learn from this? It allowed me to be soft and open with you, Dad; it let me bend with the unpredictable things that came up—the times of upset when a thought took root in your mind and you could no longer adequately communicate why you were upset. There was no guidance in those years. People didn't openly discuss Alzheimer's or its many challenges, so it was a matter of making it up as we went along. My faith got stronger—the faith you had instilled in me as a child. I asked God for guidance, and I trusted that He would soothe the places in my soul that felt bruised.

Mom, I observed you closely in those years. I could sense the widening gulf of pain in you, as communication with Dad got more and more frayed. But you never shared it. I didn't share my grief either, feeling that such interaction had to be cordoned off by a boundary line enforced by decades of practice. I would hold my tears until I was alone, often pulling off to the side of the road after I left your house to sit alone in my car and weep. I watched you try to establish yourself apart from Dad. You bravely spoke out in favor of stem cell research and treatment, neither of which was popular with the Republican Party. At one point, when there was pending legislation about stem cell research, you kept yourself busy calling senators and congressional representatives, lobbying for the legislation. It seemed to give you purpose.

One day when I went to your house, you were midway through your list of calls to elected officials and you looked at me with a bit of frustration, pointing to the phone. "I think Dick Cheney, or someone like that, is dogging my phone calls," you said.

"*Dogging* your phone calls?"

"Yes. Every time I call someone, they've either already gotten a call from someone in the White House, or they get one right after. I asked the Secret Service to see if my phone is tapped."

"Okay," I said. "And what did they find?"

"They said it isn't. But this is just very strange."

I was struck by the fact that you weren't fuming, as I would have expected. "This must be making you furious," I said.

You shook your head, straightened your shoulders, and gave me what I can only describe as a rather Zen response. "No, no time for that. I just have to keep putting one foot in front of the other."

I couldn't help myself. I said, "Okay, who are you and what have you done with my mother?" But I don't think you heard me, because you were already dialing another number.

<del>-<-->-</del>

I WATCHED YOU at the moment of Dad's death, when he opened his eyes and looked straight at you, pushing past the disease to have what I believe was one last lucid moment with you. I saw the overwhelming love and loss that would forever define your life on this earth.

I watched you in the months and years after his death, how you often seesawed between an old pattern of harshness—at least toward me—and vulnerability, which you never seemed comfortable with. I kept wondering what our lives might have been like—what you might have been like—if our family hadn't been broken into pieces so long ago.

-<-+->-

OUR PARENTS RESIDE within us. No matter how long they have been gone, or how much we have worked on processing those relationships, they occupy a good portion of our inner landscape. Sometimes I stumble across photographs of the two of you that I haven't seen before, especially older ones from when you were young and first dating. It just seems impossible to separate you. But as united as you were, as locked in your own planetary orbit as you were, inside me you live in different places.

Mom, when I think of you, I stumble over questions about why motherhood was such an unwelcome burden, why it was never infused with gratitude. There were moments of love, but I have to search a wide map to find them. When I think of myself as your daughter, I see a young girl sitting at a window peering out at a world she doesn't feel part of. You used to say you weren't afraid of death because you believed you would see Dad again. I hope you have been reunited, and I hope you are at peace.

◄◄─►►

DAD, WHEN I DRIVE to our old neighborhood and walk up the hill where we used to fly kites, I feel like you're close by, on the other side of the wind. No one ever came with us on those afternoons; the time was ours alone. The sky was blue and endless as our kite danced at the end of the string that you held with hands I believed could do anything. When I come back to these streets, the memories are all around me, whispering like a benediction.

We return to the places we once knew, to remember—to listen for echoes, and there are always echoes. The sound of bicycle tires on pavement, a child singing off-key. We return as the person we have grown into, to touch again who we once were. We look through older eyes, hopefully more forgiving eyes. We see the shadows, but we can also see beyond them.

Sometimes when I look back at you, Dad, I'm looking through tears. But they aren't all tears of sadness. They are also tears of gratitude for the father you were when I was small and you taught me to trust that even the quietest prayers are heard. For the father who taught me about the pull of ocean tides, the beauty of the land, the secret lives of animals. As Alzheimer's pulled you out to deep waters, I willingly swam as far as I could to keep you in sight. Most of all, they are tears of love for a man who carried with him the ghost of his own father. I hope you were right in what you used to tell me as a child—that God hears everything. Because maybe God will let you know that I feel you brush past me sometimes on the wind, that I still look up at the moon and hear your voice. I wish I had told you more of that when you were here.

Acknowledgments

Thank you to Bob Weil for inspiring this book, and for the careful and illuminating editing. To Gina Iaquinta, Haley Bracken, Cordelia Calvert, Clio Hamilton, Fanta Diallo, and everyone at Liveright who helped with the book. Thank you to David Rambo for early readings, and for your invaluable insights. To David Kennerly for my author photo— thank you for making it fun. To Suzanne Simonetti for letting me run things past you and for your support and encouragement. To Max Boot for the research help. To Michael Reagan, Ron Reagan, and the friends who have traveled with me on this sometimes tricky journey—you will always have my love and gratitude.